142 Fun Things To Do In NEW ORLEANS

N2·FUN

written by
Karen Foulk

Into Fun Company Publications
A Division of Into Fun, Inc.
Sugar Land, Texas

147 Fun Things To Do In New Orleans
by Karen Foulk

Cover Illustrations
by Delton Gerdes
Maps by Leo Fortuno
Layout & Formatting
by Karen Foulk & Brocky Brown

Copyright © January 2000 Karen Foulk

Library of Congress Catalog Card Number
99-097184

ISBN 0-9652464-4-2

UPC 6129060004

Into Fun Company Publications
A Division of Into Fun, Inc.
P.O. Box 2494
Sugar Land, Texas 77487-2492

Printed & bound in the United States of America

Into Fun Co. Publications are available for educational, business, and sales promotional use.

Please contact:
Into Fun, Inc.
P.O. Box 2494, Sugar Land, Texas 77487-2494
Phone: 281-980-9745   Fax: 281-494-9745
www.intofun.com

With all my love,
to my husband, Don,
who had so much fun in
New Orleans, that's all he talks about.

To my wonderful children
who believe as I do — fun's important.
Michael & Amber,
Rachel,
David,
and
Rebecca.

ACKNOWLEDGMENTS

Into Fun Company would like to thank the following individuals for their contributions in making this book a success.

Bonnie Warren — for her professional advice and charm—no one knows New Orleans better

Patti Nickell — For her support and enthusiasm — she understands the need for "fun"

Merrill Littlewood — there's no better CPA in the business

Brockton Brown — for his sincere desire to see N2Fun succeed

Ken Barrow — for his legal advice and friendship

Sharon Cooper — for her friendship—there are no better friends

Jerrie Hurd — for her interest and support. I wish her success with her new novel *HoopedSnake*.

Michael Foulk — for being Into Fun Co.'s Webmaster

Wendy Nielsen — for her contributions in every way

Paul A. Greenberg — for his information about two of his favorite things, spicy New Orleans food and the comfort and hospitality of local hotels, guest houses, and bed and breakfasts.

Kathy Buck — for her thorough and speedy editing efforts

TABLE OF CONTENTS

Without this book in hand, you're going to miss some of the fun. Experience New Orleans like you've never experienced it before. This book will take you beyond Bourbon Street. You're about to discover this city's rich and diversified history and culture.

Of course in New Orleans there's no such thing as a bad restaurant. And most New Orleanians are spoiled when it comes to food. But, listed in the book are restaurants I feel you must try. These are the best of the best—and not all of them are fancy either. Don't be fooled by the appearance of the place, the funky old dives I've included serve up some of the tastiest dishes imaginable.

You'll find the zoo one of the most charming in the country. The best part is the Swamp Exhibit. See native animals in their natural habitats up close. Believe me, nothing is wilder looking then a white alligator.

If you love jazz, spend an evening at Preservation Hall. No, this isn't any concert hall—but housed in a 1750's building that's hasn't experienced much "preservation." Although it's shabby, it adds to the memorable experience. See legendary greats perform right before you're eyes. If that wets the appetite for good music, there's plenty more music venues listed in the book.

Riding the train to New Orleans is fun. Arrive feeling relaxed. The local national park service features an educational program abroad the train that you won't want to miss. Remember to ask about their *Trails and Rails* program when you make your reservations.

I want you to know that I wrote this book for you. With its easy to read format, you'll find every thing you need to know at your fingertips. I've made it very simple to use.

Now if some one asked me what were my favorite things to do in New Orleans—I'd hand them a copy of my book. Here it is. I hope you enjoy this city as much as I do. New Orleans is one of my favorite places. Take this book every where you go, and you'll see why.

Have fun in New Orleans.

Karen Foulk

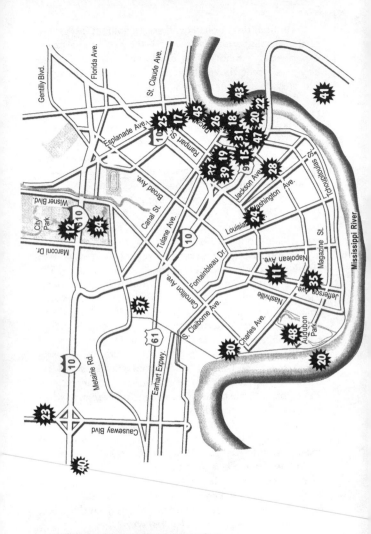

IN THE FRENCH QUARTER:

13 14 16 27 29 36 38 42 44 46

Chapter 1
WHAT'S NEW ORLEANS

Chapter 1
What's New Orleans
(continued)

ANNE RICE'S DOLL COLLECTION IN THE OLD ST. ELIZABETH ORPHANAGE

1314 Napoleon Avenue
504-899-6450

Famous author restores mid-1800s orphanage

Remember the novel *An Interview with a Vampire*, later made into a movie starring Tom Cruise? Anne Rice, the popular novelist who wrote this book and many others, lives in New Orleans. Known as the "Cities of the Dead," New Orleans' cemeteries creates a perfect setting for her famous vampires characters.

You'll enjoy touring the old orphanage. This 140-year-old building was desperately in need of repair. The author spent considerable money restoring it. The restored orphanage now houses her religious art collection, her coffin, and an extensive doll collection.

Depending on how you look at it, it's either strange or perfectly in character for a master horror novelist to house her extensive doll collection in a restored orphanage. And that's not all. The place is genuinely haunted, just ask the guide. But for serious doll collectors, the museum is an important stop. Call ahead; tours can cancel without notice.

Tour Hours
Daily . . . . 11 am, 1 pm, 3 pm

Cost
Adults $7
Children   (under 12) $5

Directions
On Napoleon Avenue at Prytania Street.

ANTIQUE CAROUSEL AT CITY PARK

Victory Avenue
504-482-4888

Ride an antique carousel with old-fashioned charm

New Orleans' show piece. In City Park, a beautiful old-fashioned wooden carousel remains one of only a few in our country. It is listed on the National Registry of Historic Places. And all ages love to ride it.

The carousel, located in Carousel Gardens inside City Park, sits under magnificent 250-year-old oaks in a lovely setting next to many other fun attractions. Be sure to take the kids and bring the camera.

Nearby attractions includes an old miniature train that has operated in the park since 1889. See City Park aboard this New Orleans keepsake.

Hours

Seasonal, May - August, call before going

Mon. - Fri. . . . . 10 am - 2:30 pm
Sat. & Sun. . . . . 11 am - 2:30 pm

Cost (Ask about discounts)

Admission $1
Ride tickets . . . . $1 each
Children under 2 year . . . . . . Free admission

Directions

City Park. From the French Quarter, take Esplanade northwest. Continue on as the street becomes Lelong Avenue and circles around the Museum of Art. Continue to Franklin D. Roosevelt Mall and immediately make a left on Victory Avenue.

BEIGNETS AT CAFE DU MONDE

800 Decatur Street
504-525-4544

New Orleans' most famous sidewalk cafe

Put Café du Monde first on your things-to-do list. That way you'll begin the day with a plate of incredibly tasty beignets. Order them with hot chocolate.

These square-shaped, puffy French Market doughnuts, dusted with powdered sugar, are a hit with tourists and locals alike. An order includes 3 beignets on a plate and your choice of milk, orange juice, hot chocolate, soft drinks, or café au lait.

Don't limit yourself to breakfast. Stop in any time of the day or night. Always crowded, the café serves fresh, hot beignets 24 hours a day. Simply plan to eat plenty of them, they're that good.

These tasty treats are so popular that many people purchase their do-it-yourself mixes for a fun get-together back home. The company store is located on 1039 Decatur, across the street from the café. A box of beignet mix costs only $2.20 and makes 4 dozen. Ask for a catalog. They ship their mixes anywhere, along with other products like regional cookbooks, t-shirts, aprons, King Cake mixes, and other things.

Hours

Closed Christmas Day

Daily . . . . open 24 hours

Cost

Plate of 3 beignets $1.20
Hot chocolate $1.20

Directions

On Decatur Street at St. Ann Street in the French Quarter.

BEST ROOFTOP VIEW OF NEW ORLEANS OMNI ROYAL ORLEANS HOTEL

621 St. Louis Street
504-529-5333

Enjoy the public viewing area on the roof at this French Quarter hotel

Take the elevator to the 7th floor. Then go left through the glass doors and follow the signs to the observation area. It sits one level above the rooftop pool. From the observation deck, you will enjoy the most spectacular view of the city and the river.

Sit awhile and enjoy the view. The roof top area has tables, chairs, and a telescope. Bring a picnic supper or some goodies to munch on. It's fun to go at night and see the city and bridge aglow.

This classy hotel's decor takes you back to New Orleans' yesteryears. Built in the 1960s, the elegant lobby has marble hallways and three magnificent chandeliers. Rooms are small, nicely decorated, and offer guests marble baths. The hotel offers 24-hour room service, a full business center, a fitness facility, valet parking, a gift shop, and a full service restaurant. The Rib Room Restaurant features excellent chicken and beef dishes in a formal setting.

Hours
Daily . . . . 7-10 pm

Cost
Observation area . . . . Free
Hotel rates . . . . $109 - 389

Directions
On St. Louis Street at Royal Street in the French Quarter.

BLOWING BUBBLES AT THE LOUISIANA CHILDREN'S MUSEUM

420 Julia Street
504-523-1357   www.lcm.org

One of the "Ten Top Children's Museums" in *Your Family* and *Parenting* Magazines

Visit one of the most popular tourist attractions in New Orleans — the Louisiana Children's Museum. Everything's educational and loads of fun.

Hoist yourself up the side of a wall using only ropes and pulleys or pick up 500 pounds by yourself with only a lever. Try throwing a basketball through a hoop while sitting in a wheelchair or blow bubbles so big you can actually stand inside them. Become a news anchor in your own news program or manage a loading dock and load cargo on a tugboat. Ride a bicycle built for two with a real skeleton and watch how your body works. Be sure to take the family here.

The museum is in an 1860s historic warehouse with over 45,000 sq. ft. of space. Present your hotel room key and get $1 off on admission. Wear comfortable clothes; plan to spend the day.

Hours

Tues. - Sat. (Mon. in summer) .. 9:30 am - 4:30 pm
Sunday . . . .   Noon - 4:30 pm

Cost

Adults / Children   (under 1 yr. - free) . . . $5

Directions

On Julia Street, between Tchoupitoulas and Magazine Streets.

BREAKFAST AT BRENNAN'S

417 Royal Street
504-525-9711

An incredible 3-course breakfast

Forget the traditional grits, biscuits, and gravy. Brennan's gives new meaning to the word *breakfast*.

Imagine sitting at a table setting with 3 spoons, 2 forks, 1 knife, and butter on a plate over a silver bowl of ice — for breakfast. Start with a bowl of their famous turtle (or oyster) soup and hot crusty French bread. The egg dishes include their Eggs Sardou or Eggs Benedict. And then there's Bananas Foster for dessert, the famous dessert invented by Brennan's.

This world-renowned restaurant is considered one of the ten best in the country. It is inside an historic 1795 mansion with all the ambiance of the Old South. Eat in the courtyard or at a table on the glassed-in terrace overlooking the courtyard.

Call for reservations and take the whole family. Brennan's is kid-friendly. It's expensive, but worth it. Purchase one of their cookbooks for some fun back home. Their newest, **Breakfast at Brennan's and Dinner, too,** has many of their favorite dishes — including Bananas Foster.

Hours
Closed Christmas Eve and Day

Breakfast . . . . 8 am - 2:30 pm
Lunch . . . . 11:30 am - 2:30 pm
Dinner . . . . 6 pm - 10 pm

Cost

Breakfast $35
Ala carte . . . . $15.75 - 35.00

Directions
On Royal Street, between St. Louis and Conti Streets in the French Quarter.

BROWSING THROUGH THE FRENCH MARKET

Riverfront

Shopping here is a tradition dating back to the Indians

Shopping at this French Quarter Market dates back to a time when the early settlers and Indians traded goods. Nowadays the fur pelts and Indians are gone, but it's still a fun place to shop for that unique item.

At this combination flea and farmers' market you can buy everything from Mardi Gras masks and leather goods to garlic ropes, nuts, or fruit in season while munching on pralines and drinking a fruit smoothie. By the way, these fresh, creamy pralines come in lots of tasty flavors: chocolate, rum, peanut butter, and pecan butter, as well as the original. It's fun to try them all.

Here's where you can purchase that one-of-a-kind souvenir, like tee shirts or mugs. Or buy dolls, sunglasses, beads, jewelry, candied pecans, boudin and andouille sausages, and hot crawfish in season. You'll find fresh spices, sauces, seafood, regional cookbooks, and much more. Booths open daily, with more merchants on weekends.

Hours

Shop hours vary

Daily . . . . 9 am - 5 pm

Directions

On the Riverfront from Barracks Street to Jackson Square. The Farmers Market runs between Barracks and Ursulines Streets.

CANAL STREET FERRY TO WEST BANK

Canal Street at the Riverfront
504-364-8114

Take a scenic ride across the Mississippi

A beautiful sunset and a pleasant glide across the Mississippi on the Canal Street Ferry definitely go together. Of course, that's not the only fun time to ride the ferry. Going after dark, with all the buildings and the bridge lighted, make the ferry one of the most romantic places in New Orleans. Or take the ferry during the day and enjoy the activity of one of the busiest ports in the world. See huge tankers, freighters, tugboats, and paddlewheelers up close. This is fun, and inexpensive.

Simply drive or walk on board and relax as you take a 25-minute ride across the river and back. Every half-hour, the ferry leaves the dock at the riverfront on Canal Street for the West Bank's historic Algiers. Remember that the last ferry leaves at 11:30 pm and returns at midnight. (Don't be caught on the west side late at night; it can be dangerous.) Cars pay for the return trip only.

Visit the only attraction on the West Bank, Blaine Kern's Mardi Gras World. A free shuttle van meets the ferry and picks up any passengers desiring a ride to the attraction and back. The last shuttle is at 4 pm. From the West Bank levee, take a look back across the river to the New Orleans skyline; it's a great view.

Hours
Daily . . . . 5:45 am - 11:30 pm
Cost
Pedestrians . . . . Free
Car/round-trip $1

Directions
At Canal St. and the riverfront.

CRAWFISH ETOUFFEE & BREAD PUDDING AT THE BON TON CAFE

401 Magazine Street
504-524-3386

Many locals list this restaurant as one of their favorites

Most tourists don't know about the Bon Ton Café, but the locals do. Here's where they go for tasty Cajun country cooking. This terrific little restaurant offers some of the best étouffée in town. Family owned and operated, the café is a favorite for turtle soup, crab étouffée, fried soft-shell crabs, eggplant shrimp, and bread pudding. And the crawfish dishes are to die for, a must-try. This is one of the few restaurants that serve crawfish year-round. Another favorite is the Crab O'Gratin — and for a good reason. You'll love eating at this off-the-beaten path café.

Only open during the week for lunch and dinner, The Bon Ton is always crowded. Dress casually, coats and ties aren't required. This is a favorite lunch place for many local business people. Reservations are taken for dinner only.

Hours

Monday - Friday

Lunch . . . . 11 am - 2 pm
Dinner . . . . 5 pm - 9:30 pm

Cost

Lunch $12.75-16
Dinner $21-28

Directions

On Magazine Street,
between Natchez Street and Poydras Street.

CRUISE FROM THE AQUARIUM TO THE ZOO

Canal Street (Riverboat)
504-586-8777 or 800-233-BOAT
6500 Magazine Street (Zoo)
504-581-4629

New Orleans has one of the best zoos; get there on a Mississippi riverboat

Catch the John James Audubon Riverboat, Canal Street, at the Aquarium of the Americas for an enjoyable 7-mile, 45-minute cruise upriver to New Orleans' world-class zoo. Aboard the riverboat, you will enjoy lots of interactive exhibits of the region's ecology while traveling one of the world's most active waterways. Offering 4 round-trip cruises daily. Call for reservations.

Step off the riverboat at Audubon Park, home to the extremely rare white (albino) alligator at their award-winning attraction, the Louisiana Swamp Exhibit. This is one of the world's only urban swamps, and it is home to lots of native critters: alligator gars, otters, snapping turtles, baby alligators, water snakes, Louisiana black bears, bobcats, and foxes to name just a few. See them up close in their native habitats.

While watching the alligators and other swamp animals, it's fun to lunch on country Cajun food at the Cypress Knee Café. Enjoy delicious red beans and rice, jambalaya, gumbo, and crawfish pie. Food here is good and inexpensive.

Other interesting places to see include the Tropical Birdhouse, the Flamingo Pond, the Sea Lion Pond, the Asian Domain, and Butterflies in Flight. See over 1000 species of butterflies in the domed facility. Ride the train to all theses major exhibits. Browse through the interesting gift shops. (Continued next page)

Riverboat Departure Hours

Aquarium . . . . 10 am, Noon, 2 pm, 4 pm
Zoo . . . . 11 am , 1 pm, 3 pm, 5 pm

Cost

One-way ticket cruise only

Adults $10.50
Children (under 12) $5.25
Children (under 2) . . . . Free

Round-trip ticket cruise only

Adults $13.50
Children (under 12) $6.75

Zoo Hours

(The last ticket is sold 1 hour before closing)
Daily   (summer weekends 'til 6) . . 9:30 am - 5 pm

Zoo Cost

Adults $8.75
Children (under 12) $4.50

Combination tickets

Round-trip ticket for cruise & zoo

Adults $19.50
Children (under 12) $9.75

Directions

Zoo: Audubon Park, on Magazine Street.

CRUISING THE MISSISSIPPI ABOARD THE NATCHEZ

2 Canal Street
800-233-2628 or 504-586-8777

An authentic steamboat cruise

See New Orleans from a different view, aboard the Natchez, an authentic sternwheeler steamboat. Take a 2-hour narrative jazz cruise down the Mississippi River, past the French Quarter, to the Chalmette Battlefield and National Cemetery. At the same time, you'll enjoy seeing the activity of one of the world's busiest ports. Great fun.

Cruises depart daily from the Toulouse Street Wharf across from Jackson Square. Boarding begins 30 minutes before departure. Daily at 11 am and 2 pm, just before the Natchez departs (except Sunday mornings), you'll hear music coming from the boat's 32-note steam pipe organ—known as a steam calliope. This free concert lasts about fifteen minutes. Records of these steam organs date back to 1865 when the Steamboat Silver Moon, carrying freed Union soldiers home after the war, played "Home Sweet Home." Nightly dinner cruises with live Dixieland jazz music can be fun, too.

Hours - Daily

Harbor/Jazz Cruises .. 11:30 am and 2:30 pm
Nightly Dinner/Jazz .... Boards at 6 pm

Harbor/Jazz Cruise Cost
Adults (Children 6-12 — $7.25) $14.75
Dinner/Jazz Cruise Cost
Adults (Children 6-12 — $21.25) $43.50

Directions
Departs from the Toulouse St. Wharf, on the Riverfront.

DRIVING ACROSS LAKE PONTCHARTRAIN AT SUNDOWN

Lake Pontchartrain Causeway Blvd.

The world's longest over-the-water bridge

Have you ever driven across an enormous lake? Here's your chance. The causeway across Lake Pontchartrain extends for 25 miles and is especially scenic at sunset. Definitely a fun thing to do if you have a car while visiting New Orleans.

Lake Pontchartrain isn't really a lake but a 610-square-mile inland estuary—the world's largest, located at the mouth of the Mississippi River. Even though it's highly concentrated with salt, it's a favorite for boating and fishing. See pelicans, seagulls, sailboats, and tugs.

The drive across the lake at sunset can be especially fun during the months of June and July. At sunset, hundreds of thousands of purple martins swoop down all at once under the causeway where they nest.

For a good view of the birds and the lake look for these two stopping points: Sunset Point (near the north shore going northbound) and at the south shore at the southbound toll booths, access at the bridge (walkway and bike path under the bridge).

While on the North Shore, eat some of the best country French cooking at a cozy inn, La Provence, 25020 Highway 190 E., 7 miles east of the causeway (504-626-7662). It's well worth the 40-minute drive.

Hours
Open 24 Hours
Cost
Toll . . . . $3 (return trip)
Directions
I-10 to Lake Pontchartrain Causeway.

23

JAZZ BRUNCH AT COMMANDER'S PALACE

1403 Washington Avenue
504-899-8221

New Orleans' most famous creole restaurant

One of New Orleans' finest restaurants, Commander's Palace, offers the best jazz brunch in town. Weekends only.

The famous traditional Jazz Brunch includes Eggs Sardou, poached eggs on creamed spinach and a fresh artichoke bottom topped with hollandaise sauce, and Creole Bread Pudding Soufflé served with whiskey sauce. Don't leave without trying Commander's famous Bread Pudding Soufflé, known as the "queen of Creole desserts." And the Blackberry Cobbler with Creole Cream Cheese Ice Cream, in season.

Sample each of their famous soups, Turtle Soup au Sherry, Creole Gumbo du Jour, and Lobster Bisque. Jackets are recommended for brunch and dinner. Ties aren't required. No shorts or jeans.

Located in an old Victorian mansion with a lush courtyard, the restaurant is owned by a member of the Brennan family.

Jazz Brunch Weekend Hours and Costs
Saturday . . 11:30 am - 12:30 pm . . . $22-29
Sunday . . . . . 10:30 am - 1:30 pm . . . $22-29

Lunch Costs /Mon.-Fri.
Complete Lunch . . . 11:30 am - 1:30 pm . . $12-18

Dinner Costs / Nightly Seatings: 6; 6:30; 8:30; 9
Complete Dinners $26-39

Directions
Take St. Charles Ave. to Washington St. Go left 2 blocks.

JAZZ AT SNUG HARBOR

626 Frenchman
504-949-0696

Best jazz club for modern jazz, blues, and rhythm and blues

Hear top local talent perform. Enjoy the dark, cozy, intimate setting of this popular late-night jazz club. The Snug Harbor Jazz Bistro is one of the hottest music venues in town. And their food is good, too. Enjoy first-rate entertainment.

With two nightly dinner shows, at 9 pm and 11 pm, this funky place features some of New Orleans world-class musicians. Listen to Ellis Marsalis, who performs regularly on Friday nights. Others include vocalists Charmaine Neville and Germaine Bazzle. Don't miss Astral Project, Walter "Wolfman" Washington, Victor Goines Quartet, or David Torkanowski.

The club offers a simple menu and most come for the thick, juicy, charbroiled hamburgers. Reasonably priced, too. Snug Harbor also serves grilled chicken breasts and tasty jumbo fried shrimp. All entrees come with a huge baked potato. Diners can't view performing musicians, but the sound is fantastic.

Hours - Daily

Dinner ... 5 pm - 11 pm (til midnight weekends)
Music Sets .... 9 pm and 11 pm

Cost (depending upon the band)

Cover charge $8-20

Directions

West of the French Quarter in Faubourg Marigny, on Frenchman between Chartres and Royal Streets.

KILLER CREATURES FROM THE DEEP AT THE AQUARIUM OF THE AMERICAS

1 Canal Street at the River
504-861-2537

Considered one of the best aquariums in America

What you see isn't always friendly at the Aquarium of Americas, but it is fascinating. You'll see over 10,000 sea creatures swimming in hundreds of thousands of gallons of water. Some are even endangered or rare.

Ever been stung by a jellyfish? See an extensive collection of them from around the world in the Jellies exhibit. See what lives at the bottom of the muddy Mississippi. It might surprise you what's down there.

See a white alligator, a 10-foot shark, and the largest tarpon in captivity. Did you know there are warm-climate penguins? See the African penguins and the Rock Hoppers at the aquarium. See what's interesting about the Amazon Rain Forest exhibit.

Most impressive is the 30-foot tunnel made of 5 1/2 inches of acrylic. The tank holds 132,000 gallons of water and a huge variety of fish from the Caribbean Reef. Be sure to visit the gift shop filled with lots of unique items.

The Aquarium of the Americas is part of the Audubon Institute that includes the Audubon Zoo, the Entergy IMAX Theater, and the John James Audubon Riverboat. If you purchase the Audubon Adventure Passport, you'll get a discounted admission to all their attractions.

Weekdays .. 9:30 am - 5 pm (til 6 weekends)

Adults $8.75
Children under 12 .... $4.50

At the foot of Canal Street.

MAKE GUMBO, JAMBALAYA, AND BREAD PUDDING AT THE NEW ORLEANS SCHOOL OF COOKING

524 St. Louis Street
504-525-2665

Attend this nationally acclaimed cooking school open to the public

Know the difference between Creole and Cajun dishes? The New Orleans School of Cooking not only teaches regional cooking, it teaches fascinating local history and culture and helps you understand the differences. The 3-hour class is entertaining, too. A must-do for any out-of-towner.

Join others seated at tables as a local chef prepares step-by-step some popular creole dishes: gumbo, Jambalaya, and bread pudding. Learn the secrets of making a rich, dark roux, whiskey sauce, and pralines. Best of all, the class samples what the chef cooks. Come away with a better understanding of Louisiana's cuisine and have fun making these dishes at home.

One of the most delightful things to do in New Orleans, reservations are necessary.

Hours

Mon. - Sat. . . . . 10 am - 1 pm and 2 pm - 4 pm
Sunday . . . . 10 am - 1 pm

Cost

Per person $25

Directions

On St. Louis St., between Chartres and Decatur Sts. in the French Quarter.

MILE-HIGH ICE CREAM PIE AT THE CAFE AT THE PONTCHARTRAIN HOTEL

2031 St. Charles Avenue
504-524-0581 or 800-777-6193

The hotel's famous for its huge slice of pie

For an unbelievable pie-eating experience you'll never forget, stop in at the café at the Pontchartrain Hotel. Order a slice of the café's yummy Mile-High Ice Cream Pie. One slice stands higher than a whopping 10 inches tall and weighs over a pound. It's that big.

This enormous pie is made of more than a gallon of the freshest, hotel-made ice cream, consisting of chocolate, strawberry, vanilla, and peppermint ice creams. Over the top of that is a healthy layer of meringue; then comes the hot chocolate sauce.

The café, as you may remember, was the setting for several different scenes in Anne Rice's novel *The Witching Hour*. The author lives only a few blocks away in a purple-colored mansion at 1239 First Street at Chestnut. Around the corner on 2727 Prytania, the Garden District Book Shop carries limited editions and autographed copies of her books.

Hours - daily

Breakfast - lunch	7 am - 2:30 pm
Dinner	5:30 pm - 9 pm

Cost

One slice of pie	$8.95
1/2 slice	$5

Directions

On St. Charles Ave. at Josephine St. in the Garden District.

MUFFALATTAS AT CENTRAL GROCERY CO. AND DELI

923 Decatur St.
504-523-1620

This famous Italian sandwich originated here

If you hunger for one of Central Grocery's muffalattas, don't worry. They will overnight them anywhere in the U.S. Just give them three day's notice. Central Grocery, an old-fashioned mom-and-pop store, created the original muffalatta in 1906 and made Louisiana culinary history.

What is a muffalatta? It's tasty sandwich big enough for two. A large, round, crusty loaf of Italian bread is loaded with hard salami, ham, provolone cheese, and olive salad. It is Central Grocery's olive salad that makes the sandwiches so good. You can buy a bottle for the trip home.

Immigrants from Sicily came to New Orleans in the late 1800s. Their specialties were cold cuts, black and green olives, cheeses, and olive oil. It was only a matter of time before they combined these ingredients into the sandwich that's so popular in New Orleans. Best served with ice-cold root beer.

Central Grocery offers a fun selection of imported items: pastas, olive oils, spices, chocolates, chestnuts, cheeses, deli meats, and more. Enjoy browsing through their store some time when the lunch crowd dies down.

Hours

Mon. - Sat. . . . . 8 am - 5:30 pm
Sunday . . . . 9 am - 5:30 pm

Cost

Whole . . . . $7.95   Half $4.50

On Decatur Street, between St. Philip and Dumaine in the French Quarter.

OMELETS OR PECAN PIE AT CAMELLIA GRILL

626 S. Carrollton
504-866-9573

Line up out front for breakfast. It's always crowded, especially on weekends. Don't worry, they serve breakfast anytime and the food is worth the wait.

Since its opening in 1946, this '50s style diner has changed very little. No tables, no chairs. Customers sit at the counter and watch the cooks prepare the food.

This old-fashioned hamburger grill is famous for its chili omelet and pecan pie. Their specialties include a chocolate pecan pie, too. Very rich and tasty. Their pecan waffles are heavenly, too. Waffles come with a choice of yummy syrups.

Wear comfortable casual clothes and have fun.

Hours

Mon. - Thurs.	9 am - 1 am
Friday	9 am - 3 am
Saturday	8 am - 3 am

Cost

Chile Omelet	$5.38
Mexican Omelet	$6.50
Chef's Special Omelet	$6.95
Pecan Pie	$2.60
Hamburgers	$2.60

Directions

On Carrollton, between Hampson and St. Charles Streets.

PO-BOYS AT MOTHER'S

401 Poydras Street
504-523-9656

Home-style cooking at New Orleans' best

Po-boy is the king of New Orleans sandwiches. Mother's, a famous local dive, makes them so good-they're world renowned. Try one of these two-fisted feasts on French bread, piled high with anything from fried oysters to roast beef and gravy.

Mother's most popular po-boy, the "Ferdi," is a roast beef po-boy with baked ham and debris added. Debris is the gravy and the bits of beef that fall into the pan while the roast cooks. (Locals ask for the "black ham," charred sugary end pieces from hams cooked with a thick paste of brown sugar, cinnamon, and pineapple.) Mother's is also known for cooking the best hams in town. If you add Swiss cheese to the "Ferdi," it becomes a "Ralph."

Po-boys were created during the streetcar strike in the 1920s when former conductors, Bennie and Clovis Martin, promised to feed union members for free. Whenever a striker entered the sandwich shop, Bennie would yell to Clovis, "Here comes another poor boy!"

Mother's offers other tasty dishes and daily blackboard specials: Red beans and rice, gumbo, crawfish étouffée (in season), shrimp salads, jambalaya, and much more. A favorite place for locals to lunch, Food's a bit pricey. Plan to wait in line.

Hours
Mon. - Sat. . . . . 5 am - 10 pm
Sunday . . . . 7 am - 10 pm
Cost
Famous Ferdi Po-Boys (roast beef) $8
Directions
On Poydras Street at Tchoupitoulas Street.

ST. CHARLES STREETCAR RIDES THROUGH THE GARDEN DISTRICT

Canal Street at Carondelet
504-248-3900

See the Garden District from the famous St. Charles Streetcar

Very picturesque. New Orleans' streetcars are among the most photographed scenes in New Orleans. While living in the French Quarter, Tennessee Williams wrote his Pulitzer Prize-winning play, "A Streetcar Named Desire." Back then, he often rode the once operating streetcar "Desire."

Only the St. Charles line still operates. It is the oldest continuously operating railway in the world. These cars are listed on the National Register of Historic Places. The St. Charles Streetcars are a popular means of transportation for locals and tourists.

Hop aboard for a delightful sight-seeing adventure of the Garden District, as you travel down St. Charles and Carrollton Avenues. Here you'll see the beautiful, landscaped gardens of old antebellum mansions. Most are privately owned and carefully preserved.

Your journey will take you past the Audubon Park (the Audubon Zoo), Tulane and Loyola Universities. At the bend in the river, as the streetcar turns onto Carrollton Avenue, the neighborhood's appropriately known as Riverbend. At this point, you may want to hop off for lunch or a late breakfast at Camellia Grill, 626 Carrollton Avenue. Their hamburgers and omelets are the best.

Walk up a block and shop 'til you drop on Maple

Street's 6 blocks (Carrollton to Cherokee Street) of fun shops in quaint turn-of-the-century cottages. Or stop at one of the lovely, oak-shaded parks along the way for a picnic. But save room for a piece of Mile-High Ice Cream Pie at the Pontchartrain Hotel's famous cafe on the return trip back to Canal Street. The 13-mile round trip takes 1½ hours. Note: Travelers must pay fare each time they board and must have the exact change.

Hours

Operates 24 hours daily

Cost

One-way $1
Round-trip $2
Children under 3 .... Free

Directions

Catch the streetcar on Canal Street at Carondelet or at numerous places along St. Charles Street and Carrollton Avenues. Watch for the stops..

SEE THE FABERGE IMPERIAL EGGS & THE LILIES-OF-THE-VALLEY BASKET AT THE NEW ORLEANS MUSEUM OF ART

1 Collins Diboll Circle
504-488-2631

New Orleans' fantastic art museum

The New Orleans Museum of Art is considered one of the finest art museums in the South, if not the finest.

The museum's $200 million art collection comprises nearly 40,000 pieces. Highlighting their collection are the 77 fabulous Fabergé jeweled treasures on extended loan from Russia. Of those pieces, the most impressive are the three Imperial eggs and the Imperial Lilies-of-the-Valley Basket, crafted for the Empress Alexandra Feodorovna. The craftsman, Peter Carl Fabergé (1846-1920) was the master jeweler to the last czar of Russia.

The museum is known for its an extensive collection of American and French art, photography, glass, African and Japanese works. See "Portrait of Estelle," by Edgar Degas. He was the only French Impressionist to visit New Orleans. The museum's glass collection is one of the six largest in the USA.

Don't leave without a visit to the museum's unique gift shop. The museum is free on Thursdays, 10 am - noon, but stay as long as you like.

Hours (Closed Mondays)
Tues. - Sun. . . . . 10 am - 5 pm

Cost
Adults (Seniors - $5) $6
Children ages 3 - 17 . . . . $3

Directions
From the French Quarter, take Esplanade Ave. northwest to the park.

SEVEN COURSE TASTING DINNER
THE UPPERLINE RESTAURANT

1413 Upperline Street
504-891-9822

Eat at one of New Orleans' favorites

Here's one of the friendliest places in town. Not only is the food wonderful, so is the service. In fact, owner Jo Ann Clevenger greets you personally at the door.

Dining at the Upperline Restaurant is delightful. Jo Ann calls her cuisine, "Classic Creole with an Adventure." To get a sample of what she offers, order her Taste of New Orleans, a seven-course dinner with Creole and Cajun favorites. You'll sample the Duck & Andouille Étouffée w/ Corn Cakes & Louisiana Pepper Jelly; Louisiana Oyster Stew; Chicken, Duck & Andouille Gumbo; Spicy Shrimp w/ Jalapeno Cornbread; 1/4 Roasted Duck w/ Ginger Peach Sauce; Fried Green Tomatoes w/ Shrimp Remoulade, and Pecan Pie or Bread Pudding. Have fun.

Ask for a guided tour of her place. She collects lots of fascinating pieces of local folk art. I find the "Wizard" pieces fascinating. The artist sells his paintings in the Martin LaBorde Gallery, 631 Royal Street, and is thought to be the next big artist from New Orleans.

Patrons come wearing formal evening wear to blue jeans. Call ahead for reservations. Bring the family; the Upperline Restaurant is one of New Orleans finer restaurants that's kid friendly.

Hours
Wed. - Sat. . . . . 5:30 pm - 9:30 pm

Cost
Entrees . . . . $16.75 - $34

Directions
In the Uptown/University Area on Upperline, between Prytania and Pitt Streets.

SPLURGE AT HOVE PARFUMEUR

824 Royal Street • 504-525-7827

Very exclusive, Southern perfumery

Myths about Hové Parfumeur on Royal Street can make interesting conversation with the shopkeepers. Many believe this exclusive perfume business grows its own flowers out back in the courtyard, or that it uses only local flora in its products. On the contrary, essential oils for their products come from around the world. Their popular fragrances, however, are formulated on the premises.

Don't miss stopping in at Hové. Sample some of the finest perfume products in the South. Ask for their catalog. Most of their business comes from tourists who love their products and order more from home.

Mrs. Alvin Hovey-King, the original owner, created the formulas for many of Hové popular perfume fragrances back in the 30s. Two of their most popular fragrances are Tea Olive and Vetivert. You'll find samples on the counter. Ask about a lavalier, filled with your favorite fragrance and worn as a necklace. Or ask about the fans.

All fragrances come from flowers, no synthetics. These special-formulated fragrances do conjure up the South. It's a lot of fun.

Hours

Mon. - Sat. . . . . 10 am - 5 pm

Cost

Standard Line Perfumes (1 dram) $18
Luxury Line Perfumes (1 dram) $21

Directions

On Royal St, between Dumaine and St. Ann
in the French Quarter.

STROLL LONGUE VUE GARDENS

7 Bamboo Road
504-488-5488

Gorgeous gardens, elegant house, now an accredited museum and historic site

Even from the servant's quarters, the view of the gardens is spectacular. See one of most elegant gardens in our country. See how the landscaped gardens and this magnificent house go together. The outside surroundings actually complement each room's decor.

Married philanthropists Edith Rosenwald and Edgar Bloom Stern built the magnificent Classical Revival house from 1939-42. She was an heiress to the Sears fortune; he, a wealthy cotton broker with interests in real estate, minerals, and timber.

They spared no expense building their house, furnishing it, and landscaping the yard. They hired a well-known New York architectural firm, William and Geoffrey Platt, to design the house, and well-known landscape architect Ellen Biddle Shipman to design the gardens.

New to the estate is the Discovery Garden. The garden offers some first-class, hands-on activities for children. Work in the vegetable garden, walk through the bamboo tunnel, or peer through the giant hydroponics water tank. Take the kids here.

Hours — Last House Tour at 4 pm

Mon. - Sat.	10 am - 4:30 pm
Sunday	1 pm - 5 pm

Cost — (House and Gardens)

Adults	$7
Students & Children 3 and older	$3
Children under 3	Free

Directions

Take Carrollton to Palmetto Street.
Go northwest and follow signs.

SWAP WAR STORIES AT LE PETIT TOY SOLDIER SHOP

528 Royal Street
504-523-7741

Any serious history buff will find Le Petite Soldier Shop an important stop. The store carries an incredible inventory of hundreds of lead soldiers, from ancient Rome and Greece to modern Desert Storm. Soldiers stand 54 mm high or 1/32 scale. Most popular is the Civil War hero Robert E. Lee.

Six local history lovers/artists meticulously hand paint the figures for this unique, fun shop. Take your time browsing through their selection of fighting men.

Hours

Mon. - Sat. . . . . 10 am - 4 pm

Cost

$20 - $250

Directions

On Royal Street between Toulouse and St. Louis Streets in the French Quarter.

SWIMMING LAPS IN THE MARBLE TUBS AT THE OMNI ROYAL CRESCENT HOTEL

535 Gravier Street
504-527-0006
www.omnihotels.com

A favorite place to stay in New Orleans

Serious! You'll marvel at the size of their marble Jacuzzi tubs. And after a day of shopping, sight-seeing, and eating, you're ready to drop. It will definitely be one of New Orleans' finest attractions.

Newly opened, the Omni Royal Crescent Hotel occupies a refurbished 110-year-old building in the Central Business District. One block from Canal Street, the hotel is within walking distance of many major attractions. Small, it offers the charm of the French Quarter with a lot of sophisticated amenities. Yet it's off the beaten path in a quiet part of town.

Besides the unbelievable marble Jacuzzi tubs, their seven lavish suites offers state-of -the-art music systems, king-size beds, premium movies, fax machines, dual-line phone lines, VCRs, and 24-hour room service. Enjoy the Roman rooftop pool, the fully equipped fitness center, and an acclaimed restaurant on site. This swanky hotel's the tops when visiting in New Orleans. It's fun to stay here.

Cost

$109 - 225 (seasonal)

Directions

On Gravier at Camp Street.

SYMPHONIES UNDER OAK ALLEY PLANTATION'S OLD OAK TREES

3645 Highway 18, Vacherie, LA 70090
800-44ALLEY or 504-265-2151
oakalleyplantation.com

Picnic while listening to a concert at an old Southern plantation

Imagine spreading a blanket out under the magnificent 300-year-old oak trees at the Oak Alley Plantation to enjoy a picnic. While you're munching away and soaking up the beautiful surroundings, you'll be thoroughly entertained by the Louisiana Philharmonic Orchestra. Mark your calendar now to attend the "Louisiana Philharmonic Orchestra Southern Serenades" held one evening in October. Plan to take the whole family. Oak Alley's the southern plantation you see in so many photographs. It's famous for its 28 old gnarled oaks, fourteen on each side, that line the walkway in front of the elegant, Greek-revival antebellum mansion. You'll recognize the place when you see it. Many a well-known movie has been film here: *Hush, Hush Sweet Charlotte*, *Primary Colors*, and *The Long Hot Summer*. If you recall, this was Louis and Lestat's home in *An Interview with a Vampire*.

In October — Call for date and times

For 1999 it was October 10 at 3 pm

Cost

Adults 19 and older $8
Children: 6-12 . . . . . . $3   13-18 . . . . . . $5

Directions

See page 216 for directions and page 210 for a map of the Great River Road Plantations.

TAKE A MOONLIGHT CANOE TRIP THROUGH THE SWAMP AT JEAN LAFITTE NATIONAL PARK

Barataria Preserve, 7400 Highway 45, Marrero, LA 70072
504-589-2330

Get up close to a real swamp

You can't do this one in New York City, Paris, or London. In fact, this one-of-a-kind experience will be something to write home about. Anyone with an adventurous spirit can join a park ranger on a moonlight canoe trip through the swamps. We're talking snakes, frogs, raccoons, and alligators—some over 7 feet long. See them by the glow of the moon as you paddle through the cypress trees and hanging Spanish moss.

Call for a reservation. The Jean Lafitte National Historical Park and Preserve (at the Baratara Preserve) offers two trips a month, on Tuesday and Wednesday when the moon is full. Then rent a canoe from Earl's Bar (504-689-3271) just outside the park. Earl's will haul your canoe into the park to the launching site and pick it up later.

Bring along a flashlight and bug repellent. Trips last 2 1/2 to 3 hours.

Daytime canoe trips are offered on Sundays at 8:30 am, or take a ranger-guided hike every day at 2 pm. Meet at the trail head for the Bayou Coquille Trail.

Hours — Moonlight Canoe Trip
Twice a month . . . . 7 pm

Cost
Canoe Rental/per day $25

Directions
Take the bridge US Highway 90 and turn left on Highway 45. Go 7 miles to park's entrance. Will be about 30 minutes from New Orleans.

THE BELGIAN MAITRE D' AT THE BISTRO AT MAISON DE VILLE

727 Toulouse Street
504-528-9206

He remembers your name as if you were an old friend. He likes to know something about all his patrons. He's simply charming and you have to meet him. He's the Belgian-born maitre d' at the Bistro, Patrick Van Hoorebeck. And he's there every day but Wednesdays.

Now that you feel like you're at home in this tiny Parisian-style restaurant, order one of their tasty dishes from the seasonal menu. Louisianian Greg Picolo's international cuisine is fabulous. Many make coming here a priority when in town.

For lunch, the Mussels Bruxelloise will be the best you've ever tried. Always served except on Sundays, it comes with a scoop of mayonnaise on top and huge French fries. Try the venison (in season) for dinner. The fact that the tables sit so close together makes meeting other interesting people half the fun. Reservations required, jackets recommended.

The restaurant is part of the small, luxury Hotel Maison de Ville, one of New Orleans' best. One of their most popular celebrities, Tennessee Williams, stayed in room #9. Guests love to request a stay in this famous room. 800-634-1600 or 504-561-5858.

Hours
Lunch	11am - 2 pm
Dinner	6 pm 10 pm

Cost
Lunch	$9.50 - $13.75
Dinner	$19.75 - $24

Directions
Located within the hotel, on Toulouse Street, between Royal and Bourbon Streets in the French Quarter.

TOUR BLAINE KERN'S MARDI GRAS WORLD

233 Newton Street
504-361-7821

Visit the world's largest float-building studio

Mardi Gras gets bigger every year. With over a billion-dollar impact on the local economy, it's definitely New Orlean's most important event. Visit where practically all the floats used in the carnival parades are made. Artists, painters, carpenters, and designers works year round, preparing floats. See impressive, expensive floats and huge heads of famous people like Michael Jackson, George Washington, and Marilyn Monroe. Watch the video. Browse through the gift shop filled with carnival souvenirs. Bring the camera. Discounts for groups are available.

Mardi Gras World is the only attraction on the West Bank.

Hours
Daily . . . . 9:30 am - 4:30 pm

Cost
Adults (Children 3-12 — $5) $9.50
Seniors 62+ $7.50

Directions
Ride the Canal Street Ferry across the river; ferries cross every 15 minutes. Mardi Gras World meets every ferry with a free ride to the attraction, last one at 4 pm.

TRADITIONAL JAZZ AT PRESERVATION HALL

726 St. Peter Street
504-523-8939

Hear traditional New Orleans' jazz

Come early, before 7:30 pm, if you want to hear New Orleans' legendary greats perform traditional jazz music at Preservation Hall. With standing room only and just a few hard benches, not everyone will get in when the doors open at 8. If you wait long enough, however, you will get in as the night progresses. Bands perform every hour for 35 minutes with time in between for purchasing CDs and letting the crowd come and go. The hall doesn't serve food or drinks.

Preservation Hall is New Orleans' most popular jazz hall. Housed in an old 1750s building, the hall is grungy and needs repair. (This is not some fancy concert hall.) Yet jazz lovers come from around the world to hear these musicians perform. Famous bands perform, generally three every evening.

Hear jazz in its traditional form, as it was nearly a century ago. Don't expect a written program listing the evening's concert numbers. Musicians do not know what they'll play beforehand. Enjoy music that comes from the souls of men—sweet, sad, exuberant music once played in street parades, in saloons, and on river boats around the turn of the century.

Hours

Daily . . . . 8 pm - Midnight

Cost

Per person $5

Directions

On St. Peter Street, between Royal and Bourbon Streets in the French Quarter.

WALK ALONG THE MISSISSIPPI RIVER LEVEE

Moonwalk

On the river levee, near Jackson Square

Here's a fun thing to do. Rise early, about the time the sun is coming up, and take a stroll along the banks of the Mississippi River. Just behind Café du Monde, up on the levee is a wooden walkway known as Moonwalk. From here, you get a panoramic view of the river as it makes its huge crescent-shaped curve around New Orleans and the Crescent City Bridge. Watch shipping activity on the river as it begins to bustle. This Mississippi River port is one of the largest ports in the United States. This wooden walkway was named for former Mayor Moon Landrieu, who opened the Riverfront area to the public for viewing the river in the 1970s.

Sit on one of the park benches along the levee and enjoy fresh beignets and hot chocolate as the ships and tugs pass by.

Hours
Always open

Cost
Free

Directions
In the French Quarter behind Jackson Square, at the river.

WINDOW SHOPPING ON ROYAL STREET

French Quarter

One of "the" streets to shop

Wander down one of the most renowned streets in the world——Royal Street. Famous for its French Quarter charm of narrow streets, historic buildings with wrought-iron balconies, and incredible shops. Here you'll find some of the best places to shop for antiques, jewelry, silver, antiques, perfumes, and paintings. Plan to spend an afternoon browsing through these shops.

Antique shopping is a serious pastime for many locals and tourists. You can find both European and American tourists on Royal Street. In fact, you can contact a local shopping consultant to go with you on a shopping expedition. If you're into antiques and want to have someone spend the day with you, showing you where to get an extra-good buy, call Malcolm Riddle, 504-899-3027, at "Let's Go Antiquing."

The following are some fun shops to look for while window shopping on Royal Street.

A Gallery for
   Fine Photography
Waldhorn & Adler
Bergen Galleries
Crafty Louisianians
French Antique Shop, Inc.
Hanson Gallery
Hove Parfumeur, Ltd.
Importicos
James H. Cohen & Sons
Le Petit Soldier Shop

Manheim Galleries
Martin LaBorde Gallery
Moss Antiques
Raymond H. Weil Co.,
   Rare Stamps
Rodrigue Gallery of
   New Orleans
Rothchild's Antiques
Royal Antiques, Ltd.
Rumors (two shops)
Richard Russell Gallery

Hours

Tues. - Sat. (most shops) . . . . . . 10 am - 5 pm

WINDSOR COURT'S AFTERNOON TEA PARTY & $8 MILLION ART COLLECTION

300 Gravier Street
504-523-6000 or 800-262-2662

Stay at one of the ten top hotels in the world

Chic it is. And words like elegant, posh, swanky, lavish, and expensive explain it, too. For those wanting a little London without leaving New Orleans, stay at the Windsor Court Hotel.

Come for afternoon tea. It's served every day from 2-6 pm at Le Salon. Bring the kids—afternoon tea includes a children's tea party, too. Enjoy scones with clotted cream, dainty pastries, and finger sandwiches (moderately priced).

The hotel's spacious rooms with marble tubs, four-poster canopy beds, dataports, and the ultimate room service, make the hotel one of the world's tops. The Windsor Court's indoor/outdoor fitness center features an Olympic-size pool. Some of the other amenities include a hot tub, a sauna, a steam room, laundry service, 2 restaurants, 266 suites, and parking.

The lobby, decorated in rich green marbles, dark woods, oriental rugs, and fresh flowers, makes an ideal display for the hotel's $8 million art collection. Most of the art in the collection has to do with the British royal family. Hotel guests and restaurant patrons can join a tour, 3 pm on Sundays, with hotel's curator Sarah Jumel, who's also on staff with the New Orleans Museum of Art. Or simply stop by and have a look.

Eat at the Grill Room, one of New Orleans finest restaurants; black ties preferred, but jackets required.

Cost
Rooms/Suites/Penthouse . . . . . . $250 - $3000

Directions
On Gravier St., between S. Peters and Tchoupitoulas Sts.

WHERE'S THE ROMAN CANDY MAN

Garden District
504-897-3937

Tasty candy that's unique to New Orleans

Watch for the Roman Candy Man; he roams St. Charles Avenue. Sometimes he's at Audubon Park, and he's always at the zoo. Rarely is he in the French Quarter. He travels about with his mule (Rose) and cart, peddling candy to the tourists and locals. Find him. It's fun. Treat yourself to some of his goodies, made fresh daily.

What he sells is unique to New Orleans. Called "Roman Chewing Candy," The Italian taffy comes in three flavors; strawberry, chocolate, and vanilla.

The Roman Candy Man is a tradition in New Orleans dating back to 1915 and continues as a family owned and operated business.

Hours
Flexible

Cost
One stick . . . . $.50

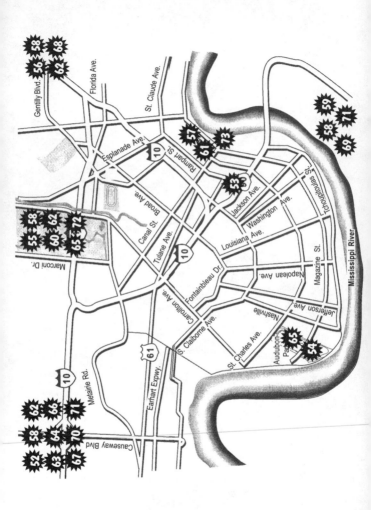

Chapter 2
OUT IN NATURE, RECREATION & SPORTS

AIRBOAT TOURS

Airboat Tours by Arthur Matherne
4438 Highway 306
Des Allemands, LA 70030
800-975-9345   504-758-1862

Over the marshes and through the swamp

Add this to your list of New Orleans adventures. Take a sunset airboat ride through an authentic cypress swamp. Airboat Tours by Arthur Matherne, 45 minutes from New Orleans near Loreauville, offers a guided tour with a local nature expert.

Any time of year is a great time to go. In the winter, view more wildlife. In the spring, enjoy the wildflowers. Summer is good for seeing an alligator. Interested in hunting? Arthur will arrange hunting or fishing trips for the fall.

Call in advance; reservations are a must. Two of his airboats accommodated 6; the other, 15. In New Orleans without a car? Call Luxury Sedans for transportation to the location (504-738-7205).

Hours

(Weather permitting; call before going)
Flexible, call for an appointment

Cost tours/person

I hour	$35
I 1/2 hours	$50
Sunset	$50

Directions from New Orleans

Take I-10 west, exit 220 (I-310) and go south. Continue 10 miles to Hwy 90 and go west. Go two miles to the yellow caution light and turn left (south) onto Hwy 306.

Go 7 miles to the yellow building # 4352 on the bayou side. It's about a quarter of a mile from the dead end.

AMTRAK'S TRAILS AND RAILS

Union Terminal, 1001 Loyola Avenue
800-872-7245

Ride Amtrak with a national park ranger

All aboard Amtrak's **Sunset Limited** for a national park ranger's narrated tour of the local countryside. You'll do more than just ride the train; you'll learn about the fascinating Acadian culture, the wildlife, and the environment of Southeast Louisiana. The joint program between Jean Lafitte National Historical Park Service and Amtrak called *Trails and Rails* takes place between New Orleans and Houston.

Catch the **City of New Orleans** and experience *Trails and Rails* all the way to Jackson, Mississippi. The program enlightens passengers on the history, culture, and natural resources of the Mississippi Delta region.

If you ride the **Crescent** between New Orleans and Atlanta, Georgia, the *Trails and Rails* program offers highlights on the Civil War and the civil rights movement.

Who could explain what you're seeing from the train better than a local national park ranger? All trains depart from Amtrak's Union Passenger Terminal located at 1001 Loyola. For more information about the program call 504-589-4428 or for fares call Amtrak at 800-USA-RAIL. These programs are growing in popularity every year.

Station Hours

Daily .... 5:50 am - 8:30 pm

Cost of fares

New Orleans to Houston, TX $47-85
New Orleans to Jackson, MI $17-33
New Orleans to Atlanta, GA $39-78

Directions

At S. Rampart in the Central Business District.

AUDUBON PARK

6500 Magazine Street
504-861-2537

Beautiful park with lots of amenities

The wildlife artist John James Audubon once lived in New Orleans. Baring his name, Audubon Park is a beautiful park covered with ancient moss-draped oaks, magnolia trees, and lush vegetation, a haven for outdoor activities. Many come every day simply to enjoy the scenery while they exercise. Audubon Park, however, offers lots of amenities: picnic shelters, gazebos, park benches, a fitness course, soccer fields, baseball fields, and a swimming pool.

Other attractions include the Cascade Riding Stables, the Audubon Golf Course, the Hermann Memorial Conservatory, and the Audubon Zoological Gardens—all first class. From the park, enjoy a spectacular view of the Mississippi River.

John Olmstead, whose father Frederick Law Olmstead laid out New York City's Central Park, designed the park in the 1890s. The park is easily accessible by the St. Charles Street Car or by the John James Audubon Riverboat, for anyone without a car. Caution: As with all parks in major cities, it's best to leave before dark.

Hours

Daily .... 6 am - 11 pm

Cost

(Each attraction charges its own admission)

Directions

The Mississippi River, Walnut St., St. Charles Ave. and Exposition Blvd. border the park. Magazine St. runs through the center.

BAYOU OAKS GOLF COURSES

City Park
1040 Fillmore
504-483-9396

Named the place to golf in New Orleans by Golf Digest

With four 18-hole courses that range from challenging to easy, any player can choose the preferred level of difficulty. The South's largest municipal golf course facility offers private and group lessons, a pro shop, and a full service restaurant at the Clubhouse Restaurant.

For those wanting to practice, the driving range opens daily from 8 am - 10 pm (504-483-9394.) Staffed by PGA pros, the Bayou Oaks Driving Range has a 100-tee, lighted double-decker facility.

Golf Course Hours

Daily . . . . 5:30 am - 6 pm (8 pm in summer)

Cost

Depending on the course

Weekdays $8-14
Weekends $12-18
Cart $18

Directions

In City Park on Fillmore Avenue,
west of Wisner Boulevard.

BAYOU SAUVAGE NATIONAL WILDLIFE REFUGE

17158 Chef Menteur Highway
504-646-7544

A 23,000-acre wetland preserve in New Orleans

Hiking, fishing, bird-watching, and canoeing make Bayou Sauvage National Wildlife Refuge a popular place for recreation. Located only 20 minutes northeast from downtown New Orleans, the wildlife refuge is still within city limits. These scenic wetlands offer some of the best fishing in brackish and saltwater. There is no charge for fishing, but you do need a fishing license. As a prime birding area, the refuge provides a bird lover's paradise. During the migratory season mid-November through mid-January, it offers free birding tours some weekends. Call for a reservation.

Hike the 1/2 mile of interpretive boardwalk to an overlook. You'll enjoy the view of the marshland, swampland, and an abundance of wildlife. Ask about the free ranger-guided canoe trips. What's nice, the refuge will even provide the canoe and necessary gear. Call for a reservation.

Hours

Daily . . . . Sunrise to sunset

Cost

Free

Directions

Within the corporate limits of New Orleans, take I-10 east and exit I-510 South. Go 1 1/2 miles. Take US 90 exit, go left (east) for 4 miles to the Ridge Trail entrance.

BICYCLE RENTALS

Enjoy the sites of New Orleans while burning off the gumbo and bread pudding. Rent a bike. Getting around New Orleans will be fun; the flat terrain makes it ideal. Ride around the French Quarter, down St. Charles Avenue, through City Park, along Lakeshore Drive, or Bayou St. John.

BICYCLE MICHAEL'S

622 Frenchman St.   504-945-9505

Rents mountain bikes geared for city riding. Caters to an adult clientele. Locks are included, helmets are $5 extra.

Hours

Mon. - Sat.	10 am - 7 pm
Sunday	10 am - 5 pm

Cost

Per hour	$5
Per day	$16

Directions

Between Chartres and Royal Sts. on Frenchman St. (Faubourg Marigny.)

FRENCH QUARTER BICYCLES

522 Dumaine St.   504-529-3136

Conveniently located in the French Quarter, they rent mountain bikes, bicycles for two, and three-speeds. Helmets and locks are part of the rental price.

Hours

Mon. - Fri.	11 am - 7 pm
Sat. - Sun.	10 am - 6 pm

Cost

Per hour	$4.50
Per day	$16.50

Directions

On Dumaine, between Decatur and Chartres Sts.

BIRD WATCHING

On a major flyway for migrating bird, these surrounding refuges and parks offer great bird watching. The refuges and parks are open to the public during daylight hours. On weekends the refuges feature free guided tours in a van, in canoes, on a hike, and even on bicycles. Call for a reservation. Also call the Audubon Society's Hot Line, 504-834-2473, for an up-to-date list, good birding places.

Bayou Sauvage National Wildlife Refuge

Migratory birds, waterfowl, and neotropical songbirds make this a popular spot for bird watching. A huge wading-bird rookery forms in the swamps from May until July. Phone: 504-646-7544

Big Branch Marsh National Wildlife Refuge

Located on the north shore of Lake Pontchartrain. Made up of winding bayous that run through pine forests, cypress swamps, fresh and salt marshes, the refuge is a haven for ducks, egrets, herons, bald eagles, and red-cockeyed woodpeckers. Access the refuge from U.S 190 and LA 434.   Phone: 504-646-7544

Jean Lafitte National Historic Park, Barataria Unit

One of the best places for birding is to walk the Bayou Coquille Trail. It begins as a hardwood forest, changes to a swamp, and ends as a fresh-water marsh. Ranger-guided walks along the trail are offered every day at 2 pm. Phone: 504-589-2330

New Orleans City Park

City Park's many lagoons and Bayou St. John (along its eastern border) attract a wide variety of birds year round. Watch for species of warblers, vireos, and passerines in the fall and spring, waterfowl in the winter, and wading birds throughout the year. Phone: 504-482-4888

BOAT RENTALS

Rent a pedal boat, canoe, or sailboat from the following. Boating on Lake Pontchartrain, or on the swamp, and bayous can be lots of fun and very scenic.

Tim Murray Sailboats

402 South Roadway Street
504-283-2507

Rent a Pearson 26-foot sailboat and enjoy sailing Lake Pontchartrain. Sailboats rent for $75 for three hours any day of the week, 9 am - 5 pm. On Sundays, it's by appointment only.

City Park

Dreyfus Avenue
504-483-9371

City Park rents canoes and pedal boats. Float in one of its many lagoons. Scenic and fun, a float through the park makes an enjoyable afternoon for any family. The boat dock sits out behind the Casino where snacks and po-boys are sold.

Open Tues. - Sun. 8 am - 6 pm weather permitting. Boats $8 per hour, $6 per 1/2 hour.

Earl's Bar (Rents Canoes)

Highway 45 at Highway 3134
504-689-3271

Rent a canoe from Earl's for $25/day and see the countryside from the water. Located just outside the Jean Lafitte National Historic Park, Earl's will deliver your canoes to the park for you. Ask at the visitor's center (504-589-2330) for places to put in.

CITY PARK NEW ORLEANS

1 Palm Drive
504-482-4888

Here's an important stop in New Orleans. Visit one of the oldest public parks in our country. With 1500 acres, it's one of the largest. The property became a public park in 1854. Although known for its ancient moss-draped oaks, see the largest stand of mature live oaks in the world. Many Creole gentlemen settled their disputes under these trees.

Ride City Park's antique wooden carousel, one of only 100 left in our country. And the miniature train has operated in the park since 1889. Both are located in the Carousel Gardens along with other fun amusement rides.

Storyland features larger-than-life fairy tales and children's characters in a playground that's one of the top ten in our country. The golfing facility, Bayou Oaks Golf Courses, and the Wisner Tennis Center are among the largest in the South. The park also offers fishing, boating, English horseback riding lessons, a softball center, a track and field facility. Be sure to see the New Orleans Botanical Gardens. Filled with lots of lush greenery, the gardens make a lovely setting for special occasions. During the Christmas holidays the park features over a million lights in the Celebration in the Oaks.

Hours
Sunrise to Sunset

Cost
Free
Admissions for attractions

Directions from the French Quarter
Take Canal St. to the cemeteries, turn right on City Park Ave. Continue until the street deadends. Turn left on Lelong Ave. to park entrance

FRENCH QUARTER GARDENS AND COURTYARDS

Most courtyards and gardens in the French Quarter are privately owned and aren't visible from the street. Here are some good destinations if lovely gardens and courtyards interest you.

Court of Two Sisters
613 Royal St.   504-522-7261

Stop in for their jazz lunch and admire their beautiful courtyard. Or simply stop in for a quick look if they're not too busy. A magnificent 100-year-old Wisteria tree forms a huge shaded canopy over the tables. This is the largest courtyard in the French Quarter.

Formal Gardens at the Beauregard-Keyes House
1113 Chartres St.   504-523-7257

Several scences for commercials, films, and the likes have been made inside the walled gardens; several movies, in the courtyard. The vegetation in the gardens remains the same as it was during its 1830s heyday, recreated from early documents. Take the tour.

Herb Gardens at the Old Ursuline Convent
1116 Chartres St.   504-529-3040

You must take the tour. These beautiful herb gardens inspired a nun to become the first pharmacist in the U.S. She wrote about the use of herbs.

Jackson Square

Once the heart of New Orleans, the square's landscaped sun pattern with walkways as rays resembles the royal gardens of Louis XIV.

Medicinal Herb Gardens, New Orleans Pharmacy Museum
514 Chartres St.   504-565-8027

This courtyard is interesting because herbs were grown here for the apothecary. Herbs were used in voodoo potions and crude medicines.

St. Anthony's Garden

Although the garden sits directly behind the St. Louis Cathedral and brings peace and tranquillity to many, it's where many a bloody duel took place.

FISHING HOLES AND GUIDES

The best fishing exists in this area. It's difficult to fish from the shores or banks because of the marshland. (Most fishing is done from a boat.) Fishing licenses can be purchased from the Louisiana Wildlife and Fisheries Department at 1600 Canal St., 504-568-5636.

City Park

City Park offers bank fishing for bass, catfish, or perch from its eight miles of scenic lagoons. Purchase any bait needed or a necessary fishing license from the park's boat dock behind the Casino where snacks and cold drinks are sold. Fishing $2/day for adults; $1/day for children under 16. Fish daily from sunrise to sundown. 504-483-9371

Lake Pontchartrain

The 5.5-mile protective seawall provides convenient fishing from Lake Pontchartrain's south shore. Fish from the steps leading into the water. No fees, but a fishing license is required

Bayou Sauvage National Wildlife Refuge

Some of the best fishing for salt-water fish happens at this wildlife refuge. There is no charge for fishing, but a license is required.

Area Fishing Guide/Charter Boat Services

Captain Brian's Bayou Adventures, Inc.
Post Office Box 13634, New Orleans, LA 70185
504-488-5581   504-895-4170(fax)
Wetland Guides & Outfitters
33132 Street Philips, New Orleans, LA 70119
504-581-3768
Fishing Guide Service
7301 Downman Road, New Orleans, LA 70126
504-243-2100

FUN PICNICS

Fresh seafood from Bucktown

Unruly kids? Need an alternative to New Orleans' fine restaurants? Don't miss out on the tasty food. Head for one of the picnic shelters along Lakeshore Drive or in City Park. On the way, pick up freshly boiled shrimp and/or crawfish along with spicy boiled new potatoes, corn on the cob, French bread, and soft drinks at one of the seafood shops that line Lake Avenue at Plaquemine St. in Bucktown. Two of the best are **Schaefer & Rusich,** 1726 Lake Avenue, and **Deanies,** 1713 Lake Avenue.

Hours

Schaefer & Rusich - Closed Monday

Tues. - Sun. . . . . 8 am - 6 pm

Deanies

Daily . . . . 11 am - 10 pm

Directions

From I-10 going west from downtown New Orleans, exit Pontchartrain Boulevard. Go north to Lake Avenue. Street goes to the left.

Italian Sandwiches/Po-Boys on the River Levee

Or pick up Italian sandwiches—especially muffalattas—Sicilian cookies, and other import goodies from the quaint neighbors **Central Grocery Co. and Deli,** 923 Decatur, and **Progressive Grocery,** 915 Decatur. Don't forget to bring along ice-cold root beer. Carry them back to Woldenberg Riverfront Park for a picnic. As you eat, enjoy watching the activity on the river.

Hours

Central Grocery Co. and Deli

Daily . . . . 8 am - 5:30 pm

Progressive Grocery

(If business is slow, they'll close early in the afternoons.)

Daily . . . . 9 am - 5:30 pm

GLOBAL WILDLIFE CENTER
26389 Highway 40; Folsom, 70437
504-796-3585

Go on a wildlife safari in a covered wagon

On the north side of Lake Pontchartrain, outside Folsom, see two thousand exotic animals, many endangered and rare, at the Global Wildlife Center. Open year round, the center's the largest for totally free-roaming animals in the United States.

Covered wagons take visitors through the open fields to view the animals up close; many animals come looking for the food they know is in the wagons. Animals include giraffes, bison, antelope, zebras, llamas, gazelles, and even kangaroos. The two humped-back camels were bottle-fed at the center. Half the fun is being out in this beautiful Louisiana countryside. Bring the kids and the camera. Tours quickly fill up on weekday mornings during the school year. Public tours begin at 1pm, 2 pm, and 3 pm. On weekends, tours start every hour on the hour on a first-come basis.

Hours
Weekdays, call for available tour times
Weekends . . . . 9 am - 4 pm

Cost
Adults $10
Children 2 - 11 . . . . $8
Children under 2 . . . . Free
Seniors 62+ $9

Directions
Take I-12 to exit 47 Robert exit and turn right onto Hwy. 455 going north. Go 11 miles and turn right on Hwy. 40 going east. Go 1½ miles and watch for entrance on the left

HORSEBACK RIDING STABLES

Cascade Stables
700 East Drive
504-891-2246

Ride a horse on the bridle paths around the edge of beautiful Audubon Park. A wonderful way to see this the park. Open to the public, for 1-hour guided trail rides or English riding lessons.

Hours
Daily .... 9 am - 4 pm
Cost
Trailride/person $20
Individual lesson $25
Group lesson $20
Directions
From the French Quarter, take Magazine Street, go left on Henri Clay Blvd. Turn right on Laurel Street to park entrance.

City Park Stables
Fillmore Avenue
504-483-9398

English riding lessons only. No trail rides. Beginners start with a half-hour private lesson. Non-beginners may choose to join a group. Call to reserve a time. Weekends are busy.

Hours
Call for an appointment
Cost
½ hour lesson $25
Directions
In the northeast end of City Park,
on Fillmore Avenue at Marconi Drive.

KLIEBERT'S TURTLE AND ALLIGATOR FARM

41067 West Yellow Water Road
Hammond, LA 70401
800-854-9164   504-345-3617

Experience the Louisiana countryside

Venture northwest of New Orleans to this one-of-a-kind turtle and alligator farm. For 35 years the Kliebert family has raised thousands of turtles and alligators each year, Turtle hatchlings from the eggs laid in dirt nests on pond banks are shipped overseas for children's pets and for food. Young alligators in pen await their turn to be sold to hide, restaurant, and breeding stock markets.

Take the guided tour of this unique farming operation. See alligators over 16 feet long, weighing over 1200 pounds. Watch them feed the alligators and harvest the eggs. Mother alligators fiercely protect their eggs. Browse through the gift shop.

Hours

Open March 1 - November 1
Weather permitting/Closed holidays

Daily . . . . .Noon - 7 pm

Cost for guided tour

Adults $6
Children $3
Seniors (62+) $4

Directions

Located 50 miles from downtown New Orleans. From New Orleans, take I-55 North to the Springfield exit. Cross over LA 22 West and turn right onto the freeway service road going north. Follow the signs.

LAKESHORE DRIVE
Lake Pontchartrain

Drive Lake Pontchartrain's scenic south shore

Drive along Lake Pontchartrain's scenic south shore on Lakeshore Drive. The road hugs the levee for 5½ miles from the West End Park to the University of New Orleans East Campus. You will encounter numerous parks and picnic shelters. A protective wall now stands in what was once a marshland. Built in the 1930s, wall extends into the lake with concrete steps, making it a fun place to sit and watch the sunset.

The wall invites a power walk, stroll, or bicycle ride. You'll find the locals fishing and crabbing from the shore. The wall protects one of the most expensive residential areas in the city (Lake Vista.)

Hours

Daily . . . . 8 am - 10 pm

Directions

From downtown, take I-10 west and exit West End Blvd and go (left) north on West End Blvd. Continue as the street becomes Lakeshore Dr.

LOUISIANA NATURE CENTER

Joe W. Brown Park
Read Boulevard at Nature Center Drive
504-246-5672

An arboretum in New Orleans

Celebrate nature New Orleans' style. Only at the Louisiana Nature Center's gift shop can you find tee shirts with nutria on the front or other unique items having to do with the local environment. This 86-acre bottomland hardwood preserve, located within New Orleans' urban community, keeps city folks in touch with their environment.

Hike one of the nature trails. Visit the greenhouse teaching center or the Interpretive Center, which features a Discovery Loft on the 2nd floor with shells, rocks, skeletons, fossils. Watch as the squirrels, butterflies, rabbits, and birds feed at the Wildlife Gardens. See alligators, herons, ducks, fish, and egrets. One of the most scenic times to go is when the iris is in bloom.

The planetarium features shows daily and concerts on Friday and Saturday nights. 504-246-STAR

Hours
Closed Mondays

Tuesday - Friday	9 am - 5 pm
Saturday	10 am - 5 pm
Sunday	Noon - 5 pm

Cost

Adults	$4.75
Children (2 -12)	$2.50
Seniors (65+)	$3.75

Directions

From I-10 traveling east towards Slidell (about 8 miles from the French Quarters) exit 244. Go right on Read Road. The center is located east of Read Road, three lights down. Watch for signs.

LOUISIANA SWAMP TOURS

Impress yourself with an alligator. Either of these swamp tours offers narrated guided tours in a nearby authentic Louisiana swamp. Don't forget the camera.

Cypress Swamp Tours

501 Laroussini, Westwego, LA 70094   504-581-4501

Take a covered boat ride through Bayou Segnette, 12 miles from downtown New Orleans. Shuttle rides from your hotel are free or drive yourself. Tours last 2 hours. Reservations required. Browse through their unique gift shop housed in an 1897 Creole cottage loaded with handcrafted items.

Tours
Daily .... 9:30 am, 11:30 am, 1:30 pm

Cost
Adults $20
Children (6 - 12) $12

Directions
From downtown New Orleans, take Hwy. 90 across the river. Stay on the elevated West Bank Expressway in the leftmost lane. Go 6 stoplights to Louisiana St. and turn left. Go one block. Park in front of the Cottage Gift Shop.

Honey Island Swamp Tours
504-242-5877

A wetland ecologist personally guides nature tours through the wilderness swamps of Honey Island. The 250-square-mile island, a 70,000-acres wildlife sanctuary, is located 45 minutes from downtown New Orleans. See an abundance of wildlife: alligators, turtles, herons, egrets, pelicans, and nutrias in their nature environment. Hotel shuttle extra.

Daily tours .... 8:30 am - 1:30 pm

Cost
Tour only
Adults $20
Children under 12 .... $10

MICKEY RETIF COCONUT BEACH VOLLEYBALL COMPLEX

7360 W. Roadway
West End Park
504-286-0333
www.coconutbeachnola.com

Popular volleyball complex near Lake Pontchartrain's south shore

The complex fills every night from March through November with locals playing volleyball. Anyone is welcome to play if the sand-filled courts aren't being used for tournaments or leagues. Bring your own ball. The Coconut Bar & Grill will lend you a ball.

Several pro volleyball competitions are held here each year. Many come to watch. Indoor leagues and tournaments held during the winter. Check their website for the schedule of events.

Hours

(Summer)

Daily . . . . 4 pm - Midnight

Cost

Free

Directions

Located in West End Park. From I-10, exit West End Blvd. and go north on West End Blvd for 1.4 miles. Continue on Lakeshore Dr. and turn left at Lake Marina Dr. (it will become W. Roadway St.).

STATE PARKS NEAR NEW ORLEANS

If you like camping, boating, birding, fishing, hiking, and picnicking, take a look at the following state parks not far from New Orleans.

Bayou Segnette State Park

7777 Westbank Express
Westwego, LA 70094
540-736-7140 or 888-677-2296

Beautiful marshland environment. See an abundance of wildlife. Offers great fishing and a bird lover's paradise. Amenities include 20 waterfront cabins, 98 campsites, picnic tables, a boat ramp, a playground, and a wave pool. Twelve miles from New Orleans, take I-10 across the river and exit Business 90 (Westbank Expressway). Follow for several miles; will be on the left.

Fairview Riverside State Park

P.O. Box 856 Highway 22
Madisonville, LA 70447
504-845-3318 or 888-677-3247

Situated on the banks of the Tchefuncte River, 1 mile east of Madisonville on Highway 22. With boating access to Lake Pontchartrain, the park offers 81 improved campsites, excellent fishing, canoeing, picnicking, and a playground. Huge live oaks.

Fontainebleau State Park

P.O. Box 8925 Highway 190
Mandeville, LA 70470
504-624-4443 or 888-677-3668

Overlooking the north shore of Lake Pontchartrain. Fontainebleau State Park is located on Highway 190, 2 miles southeast of Mandeville. Offers picnic sites, grills, 127 campsites, a swimming pool, sandy beaches. Also has fishing, nature trails, and a playground.

WISNER TENNIS CENTER

City Park
Victory Avenue
504-483-9383

Named one of the 25 best municipal facilities in the nation by Tennis Magazine

Tennis anyone? The city of New Orleans offers the public one of the largest tennis facilities in the South. Located in City Park, the facility has 35 lighted outdoor courts and a pro shop. Individual and group lessons, too. Didn't bring your racquet? They rent them for $3/hour. Call and make a reservation. During the day, any weekday is a great time to find an empty court.

Hours

January through February

Daily .... 7 am - 7 pm

March through November

Mon. - Thurs. .... 7 am - 10 pm
Fri. - Sun. .... 7 am - 7 pm

December

Daily .... 7 am - 5 pm

Cost

Per person/hour $5.50
After 6 pm/per person $6.50

Directions

Inside City Park on Victory Avenue, across from Storyland.

WOLDENBERG RIVERFRONT PARK

Riverfront

New Orleans' newly renovated riverfront park

Not only does Woldenberg Riverfront Park let you view the mighty Mississippi River, it offers a haven from the hustle and bustle of the city. Escape with a muffalatta or a po-boy sandwich for few moments of peace and relaxation. At the same time, watch the activity on one of the busiest waterways in the world. Enjoy the variety of trees, lush vegetation, and landscaping that are part of the city's recent renovations.

Woldenberg Riverfront Park is also an important stop for art lovers. The outdoor sculpture garden features major artworks of well-known artists. Enjoy the sounds of the many freelance musicians that frequent the park.

Hours

Mon.-Thurs. & Sunday .... 6 am - 10 pm
Friday and Saturday .... 6 am - Midnight

Cost

Free

Directions

On the Mississippi levee,
between Toulouse and Canal Streets.

IN THE FRENCH QUARTER:

76 • 78 • 79 • 83 • 84 • 87 • 90 • 91 • 93 • 94 • 96 • 98 • 99

Chapter 3
HISTORIC SITES AND MUSEUMS

1850 HOUSE

523 St. Ann
504-568-6968

Mid-19th-century family life in the French Quarter

Ever wondered what antebellum life in the French Quarter was like? You'll have a better idea once you visit the 1850 House.

Located around the corner from the Cabildo, the 1850 House is part of the Louisiana State Museum that includes the Cabildo, the Presbytere, and the U.S. Mint. See a re-creation of a mid-19th century, middle-class creole household and get a rare look into New Orlean's most affluent period.

The three-story rowhouse—a National Historic Landmark—is one of two belonging to the Baroness Micaela Almonester de Pontalba. She designed and built them based on French architecture of the period, adding style to this important part of town—Jackson Square. Take notice of the famous iron grillwork with the Baroness's initials imbedded into the design.

Set up as it was back then, the ground floor, once used for commercial tenants, now houses the museum's gift shop. The upper levels rented to residential tenants.

Ask about the discount combination ticket that's good for any of these historical sites.

Hours

Tues. - Sun. . . . . 9 am - 5 pm
Tours . . . . 11 am, 1 pm, 3 pm

Cost

Adults $3
Seniors & Students with ID $2
Children under 12 . . . . Free

Directions

On St. Ann Street between Decatur and Chartres Streets in the French Quarter.

AMERICAN ITALIAN RENAISSANCE MUSEUM

537 S. Peters Street
504-522-7294

Understand the Italian community's influence on the culture of New Orleans

The large Italian community has contributed much to the city of New Orleans. See the Italian influence at the American Italian Renaissance Museum. Besides highlighting their contributions, the museum serves as an archive for immigration records and as a research library. Ask to go on the tour.

The museum is located on the S. Peters Street side of the Piazza d' Italia, a square designed after post-modern Roman ruins. Browse through the interesting shops.

Hours
Wed. - Sat. . . . . 10 am - 3 pm
Tours . . . . 10 am - 2:30 pm

Cost
Free

Directions
On S. Peters, between Poydras and Lafayette in the French Quarter.

BEAUREGARD-KEYES HOUSE AND GARDEN

1113 Chartres Street
504-523-7257

Former residence of two world-famous New Orleanians

What do a famous romance writer and a well-respected Confederate General have in common? They both were tenants of the same house built in 1826 by a wealthy auctioneer, Joseph Le Carpentier. Rooms were rented in 1865 to Confederate General PGT Beauregard in the 1940s to novelist Francis Parkinson Keyes. She wrote many of her beloved novels while living here. She's the author of such favorites as *Dinner at Antoine's, Chess Player, Steamboat Gothic,* and *The Blue Camellia.* Browse through the gift shop for copies of her books.

Take a tour of this magnificent raised cottage with a Greek Revival entry and manicured French gardens. Stories of ghosts, particularly of General Beauregard looking for his boots, make the tours all the more interesting during the Halloween season.

Hours

Mon. - Sat. . . . . 10 am - 3 pm

Cost

Adults $5
Seniors and Students (13-18) $4
Children (6-12) $2
Children under 6 . . . . Free

Directions

On Chartres, between Governor Nicholls and Ursulines in the French Quarter.

CABILDO

701 Chartres
504-568-6968

Early Louisiana history portrayed

Here's where the transfer of the Louisiana Territory to the U.S. took place, December 20, 1803, in the counsel chamber on the second floor. See interesting displays on Louisiana's history from early colonial times, the Civil War, and throughout the Restoration.

This historical landmark looks very much like the building—the Presbytere—on the other side of the St. Louis. These buildings now belong to the Louisiana State Museum. And the name Cabildo? The building once housed the Spanish governing council, the Illustrious Cabildo, from 1799-1803. Fire damaged the building in 1988, but many important artifacts were saved: Napoleon's death mask and artifacts from the Mississippi steamboats, plantations, and slavery. See a slave auction block. The museum houses many interesting artifacts from the Battle of New Orleans, such as a lock Andrew Jackson's hair.

The Cabildo is part of the Louisiana State Museum, including the Old U.S. Mint, the Presbytere, and the 1850 House. Ask about the discount combination ticket that's available for all three attractions.

Hours
Tues. - Sun. .... 9 am - 5 pm

Cost
Adults $5
Seniors & Students with ID. $4
Children under 12 .... Free

Directions
In Jackson Square on Chartres Street at St. Peters Street in the French Quarter.

CHALMETTE BATTLEFIELD AND NATIONAL CEMETERY

8606 W. St. Bernard Highway
504-589-4430

The Battle of New Orleans

Visit the site of the Battle of New Orleans. Here General Andrew Jackson led his makeshift army of local volunteers and Tennessee sharpshooters against a well-trained British army. The battle took place January 8, 1815. When it was all over, the Redcoats were defeated and the city was spared.

Many claim the victory was due to Jean Lafitte's last-minute assistance. Others say it was the Ursuline nuns' prayers. Whatever the case, a draft of the the Treaty of Ghent had been signed two weeks earlier. It was still an important moral victory.

Every year, the nuns hold mass on that day to thank God for delivering them, just as they had promised God they would do. Also every year, the battle is commemorated as living history.

Walk the grounds, read the historic markers, and climb on the levee for a view of the river. An important stop for any history buff.

Hours

Daily .... 9 am - 5 pm

Cost

Free

Directions

In Chalmette on St. Bernard Highway (Hwy 46). From the French Quarter, take Rampart going northeast to St. Claude Avenue. Continue on St. Claude Avenue as it turns into Highway 46. Continue 1/2 mile. It will be on the right.

CONFEDERATE MUSEUM

929 Camp Street
504-523-4522

See many interesting Civil War artifacts

The Confederate Museum—any history buff's idea of fun. Visit the place where Confederate President Jefferson Davis's body lay in state (in the Memorial Hall) before being buried in Richmond, Virginia. See many of his personal effects, given to the museum by his wife.

The museum, more than a hundred years old, is Louisiana's oldest. Designed in 1891, this unique Romanesque building was built by the famous architect Thomas Sully. Note the large iron cannon (an 8" Columbiad) out front. It is dedicated to the 13 men killed or wounded near it during the Union siege at Mobile, Alabama.

Inside the museum, you'll find the 2nd largest collection of Confederate memorabilia in our country, after the collection in Richmond, Virginia. The collection consists of 5 Confederate generals' uniforms, personal artifacts from Louisiana Confederate soldiers, swords made in New Orleans, restored battle flags, antique guns, and artillery. Be sure to browse through the gift shop filled with souvenirs and many rare books.

Hours

Mon. - Sat. . . . . 10 am - 4 pm

Cost

Adults $5
Seniors and Students with ID $4
Children 7 - 12 . . . . $2

Directions

On the corner of Camp St. and Howard Avenue.

EDGAR DEGAS HOUSE

2306 Esplanade
504-821-5009 or 800-755-6730

Degas painted in New Orleans

Edgar Degas, the only painter of the French Impressionists ever to come to the United States, came to visit his uncle's family. His mother was a native of New Orleans. During his five months' stay from October 1872 to April of 1873, he created some of his most impressive paintings. From the 17 paintings he did in New Orleans, his "Cotton Office in New Orleans" was his first to be purchased by a museum. And his "Portrait of Estelle," in Impressionist style, is one of his most popular and best known.

As his eyesight began to fail, Degas set up his studio in his uncle's house in the heart of the French community in New Orleans. Tour the house and see where he painted virtually the entire body of his New Orleans collection. Watch the interesting video of his time and family. And be sure to browse through the gift shop. The tour lasts about an hour and a half.

Built in 1852, the house now displays 65 prints of his works. It is listed on the National Registry of Historic Homes and also serves as a bed and breakfast.

Hours

Mon. - Fri. . . . . 10 am - 3 pm
Sat. - Sun. . . . . 10 am - 4 pm

Cost

Adults $10
Seniors $9
Children under 12 . . . . $5

Directions

On Esplanade Street at N. Tonti Street.

GALLIER HOUSE MUSEUM

1118-1132 Royal
504-525-5661

Take a tour of famous architect's home

James Gallier, Jr., New Orleans' famous architect, built his home in 1857. Today, great effort has gone into restoring it. Furnished in the splendor of its day, the home is now one of New Orleans' finest historical landmarks. See one of the best-preserved houses in the French Quarter.

The Creole-style mansion offers visitors a peek into the past. The home site includes an interior courtyard and slave quarters.

As you tour the home, note the latest in 19th-century conveniences: a hot water system, an air-ventilation system, and gas-burning lights. Enjoy checking out the gift shop.

Hours

Tours 10,11,12,1:30,2:30,3:30
Mon. - Sat. . . . . 10 am - 4 pm

Cost

Adults $6
Children 8 - 18 . . . . $4
Children under 8 . . . . Free
Seniors $5

Directions

Located on Royal Street, between Ursulines and Governor Nicholls in the French Quarter.

HERMANN-GRIMA HISTORIC HOUSE

820 St. Louis Street
504-525-5661

French Quarter living in New Orleans' Golden Age

This two-story brick mansion, built 1831 for Samuel Hermann, reflects the elegant lifestyle of prosperous Creole families before the Civil War. Because of the panic of 1837, Hermann was force to sell his home in 1844 to Felix Grima. Grima's family lived in the house for five generations, until 1921. The Women's Exchange now owns it. The house opened in 1971 as an accredited museum and National Historic Landmark.

Tour the house. Meticulously restored, the Hermann-Grima House remains one of the most elegant houses in the French Quarter. The rear gallery facing the courtyard is very impressive.

On Thursdays, from October through May, visitors enjoy watching experts cook authentic period dishes in the old 1831 kitchen. Visitors sample the food and take home recipes for their own experiments at home.

Hours

Monday - Saturday	10 am - 4 pm
Tours	10,11,12,1:30,2:30,3:30

Cost

Adults	$6
Children 8 - 18	$4
Children under 8	Free
Students & Seniors 65+	$5

Directions

In the French Quarter on St Louis, between Bourbon and Dauphine Streets.

HISTORIC BUILDINGS IN THE FRENCH QUARTER

Not open for tours, (except the Madame John's Lagacy cottage) these famous buildings are still worth noticing. Look them up as you wander about the French Quarter.

Cornstalk Hotel
915 Royal Street

Every day, people stop to admire the cast iron fence in front of this small hotel on Royal Street. A work of art, the fence of corn stalks and morning glories was a present to the former owner's wife, who missed living in the country. Built in 1850.

Faulkner House
624 Pirates Alley 504-524-2940

William Faulkner, the Pulitzer Prize-winning author, lived here as he wrote his first novel, *Soldiers' Pay*. Now the former townhouse is a bookstore with many of his first editions and other rare findings.

Madame John's Legacy Cottage
632 Dumaine (between Chartres and Royal)

Many claim this small raised cottage is the oldest home in New Orleans, a good example of French West Indies architecture. One of George Washington Cable's short stories influenced its name. Self-guided tour.

Louisiana Supreme Court Building
400 Royal Street

Still being renovated, this noticeable landmark, built in 1907, once served as the Civil Courts Building and then the Louisiana Department of Wildlife and Fisheries. It was abandoned for years and has been under renovation since 1992. It will house the Louisiana Supreme Court when finished.

HISTORIC HOMES ALONG ST. CHARLES AVENUE AND IN THE GARDEN DISTRICT

You can't help but admire the beautiful old mansions in the Garden District. Not open to the public for tours, the following will grab your attention as you drive or walk pass then.

Dabney-O'Meallie House
2265 St. Charles (at Philip St.)

Built in 1857 by the famous architecture James Gallier who had a home on Royal Street. It's Greek Revival style.

Wedding Cake House
5809 St. Charles St.

Notice the entryway, the beveled leaded glass door, and the fancy balconies. See how it earns its nickname.

Payne-Strachan House
1134 First St. (at Camp St.)

Confederate President Jefferson Davis died at this house while visiting his friend Judge Jacob Payne. Built in 1849, the Greek Revival house was a first for ornamental ironwork.

Robinson House
1415 Third St. (at Coliseum St.)

Formerly owned by a tobacco merchant, Walter G. Robinson, the house is one of the most elegant in the Garden District.

Colonel Short's Villa
1448 Fourth St. (at Prytania St.)

Henry Howard designed the Short's Italianate mansion with the Cornstalk Fence—one of two originals (the other is at 915 Royal Street)—and the Nottoway plantation house.

HISTORIC NEW ORLEANS COLLECTION

533 Royal Street
504-523-4662

Museum/research center for local history

What's uniquely New Orleans? The Historic New Orleans Collection makes a great beginning. Stop here for an understanding of New Orleans architecture, history, and culture. See the city's finest collection of historic records.

Two private collectors of Louisiana materials, the late General Kemper Williams and his wife Leila bought the Merieult House and started the Historic New Orleans Collection. The Merieult House, built in 1792, survived the great fire of 1794 and remains one of only a few from the Spanish Colonial period. As their private collection continued to grow, the owners' wished to make it available to the public.

The 35-minute tour takes you through the Williams' residence. The 45-minute history tour takes you through 10 different galleries. See original maps, rare books, important manuscripts, and documents on display. Also see documents on Colonial Louisiana, the Louisiana Purchase, the Battle of New Orleans, Civil War history, and much more.

Tour Hours
Tues.- Sat. . . . . 10 am, 11 am, 2 pm, 3 pm

**Cost (Children under 12 are admitted
in the gallery and on the history tour only)**
Adults & Children over 12 . . . . $4

Directions
In the French Quarter on Royal St.,
between Toulouse and St. Louis St.

HOUSE OF BROEL'S VICTORIAN MANSION AND DOLLHOUSE MUSEUM

2220 St. Charles Avenue
504-525-1000 800-827-4325

Miniature dollhouses on display in Garden District mansion

Visit a museum of miniature dollhouses, displayed inside a historic mansion that serves as a private home. The owner, Bonnie Broel, a Polish countess and world-renowned fashion designer, assembles the dollhouses and meticulously decorates them. See many different styles of dollhouses: plantation, Victorian, Tudor, and more. Some are antiques.

Tour the house. Built in the 1850s, this three-story antebellum mansion filled with beautiful antique furniture was once only a two-story mansion. In the 1890s, the owner, a tobacco millionaire named Simon Hernsheim actually had the house lifted and another first story built in place. The house is an excellent example of high Victorian architecture.

Hours

Tues. - Sat. . . . . 10 am - 6 pm

Cost

Adults and Children $5
Children 12 mos. or younger . . . . Free

Directions

On St. Charles Ave. at Jackson Ave.

JACKSON BARRACKS MILITARY MUSEUM

6400 St. Claude Avenue, Building 201
504-278-8242

Learn about the history of Louisiana

President Andrew Jackson built the Jackson Barracks during his administration to house the federal troops needed to defend New Orleans from invasion via the Mississippi River. Both Robert E. Lee and Ulysses S. Grant served time here (from 1844-1846) as lieutenants. Other famous men to have visited or served at the Jackson Barracks were Confederate General P.G.T. Beauregard and Union General George B. McClellan; future President Zachary Taylor; American statesman Henry Clay; and World War I Commander in Chief General John J. Pershing.

In 1955, the State of Louisiana purchased the Jackson Barracks. It now serves as the headquarters for the Louisiana National Guard and the Louisiana Army.

Visit the Jackson Barracks Military Museum, with a nice collection of uniforms, weapons, flags, and other memorabilia from the Revolutionary War to Desert Storm. The grounds around the barracks include many interesting military vehicles and aircraft.

Hours
**(Closed on many holidays &
sometimes the Saturday before the holiday)**

Mon. - Fri. . . . . 7:30 am - 4 pm
Saturday . . . . 9 am - 3 pm

Cost
Free

Directions

Take N. Rampart east (it turns into St. Claude). Cross over the Industrial Canal Bridge. Continue about 1/2 mile further.

JEAN LAFITTE NATIONAL HISTORICAL PARK AND PRESERVE

Visitors' Center
419 Decatur Street
504-589-2636

Take a guided tour of the French Quarter with a park ranger

Bet you didn't know the French Quarter has a national park visitor center? Named after the notorious pirate Jean Lafitte, the Jean Lafitte National Historical Park and Preserve is unusual in that it's made up of different units: the French Quarter Unit, the Chalmette Unit, the Barataria Preserve, and others.

The Visitors' Center offers visitors a glimpse into the different ethnic groups that settled in this area and a nifty gift shop.

Be sure to get a pass for the free daily walking tour of the French Quarter. Passes are given out promptly at 9 am. The tour begins at 10:30 am. and is led by one of the rangers. Wear comfortable shoes. Definitely a fun thing to do in New Orleans.

Hours
Daily .... 9 am - 5 pm

Cost
Free

Directions
In the French Market on Decatur Street, between Conti and St. Louis Sts.

MUSEE CONTI HISTORICAL MUSEUM
917 Conti
504-525-2605

New Orleans history in a wax museum

Step into the dark, cool environs of this wax museum for a look into New Orleans' 300-year past. The translucent qualities of the wax and layers of colors create life-like appearances. See colorful historical characters like the pirate Jean Lafitte, Voodoo Queen Marie Laveau, Mardi Gras Indian Chief Montana, Louis Armstrong, and Andrew Jackson. You'll also meet up with some spooky folks in the chamber of horrors: Frankenstein, the Wolf Man, Dracula, and more.

Made in Paris, the wax figures' eyes come from Germany and the hair from Italy. Note the intricate details in the costumes. Many of the weapons used are antiques, others replicas.

Hours
(Closed Christmas and Mardi Gras)

Mon. - Sat. . . . . 10 am - 5 pm
Sun. . . . . Noon - 5 pm

Cost

Adults $6.75
Students with ID $4.75
Children $5.75
Seniors $5.75

Directions

Located on Conti between Dauphine and Burgundy Streets in the French Quarter.

NATIONAL D-DAY MUSEUM

945 Magazine Street
504-527-6012

New Orleans' new museum preserves important artifacts

It all happens on the 56th anniversary of the Normandy Invasion—June 6, 2000—the opening of the new National D-Day Museum. The Museum, honoring the men and women involved, will highlight the days when England, Canada, and the United States invaded the beaches of Normandy in World War II. History buff or not, you'll enjoy this one-of-a-kind museum.

Many interesting artifacts from the battle on Utah and Omaha Beaches will be on display. See German vehicles, sentry boxes, weapons, and equipment used from both sides of the war. See the reproduction of the Higgins Landing Craft. The museum will feature an academy award-winning film *D-Day Remembered,* four interactive galleries, and nine oral history stations. The Invasion of Normandy is considered the most complex military operation ever staged.

Hours

(Closed Thanksgiving, Christmas, New Years and Mardi Gras)
Daily .... 9 am - 5 pm

Cost

TBA

Directions

In the Warehouse District on Magazine Street at Howard Avenue.

NEW ORLEANS
HISTORIC VOODOO MUSEUM
724 Dumaine Street
504-523-7685

New Orleans' dark side revealed

What most people know of the voodoo religion, they learned from the movies. The New Orleans Historic Voodoo Museum will attempt to change your perception of this religion. Then again, maybe it won't. Interesting. Unsettling.

Not for everyone. Take a peek at the back rooms, lead by a practicing witch. See lots of crude, handmade icons, a human skull, a petrified cat, altars, and love potions. As your guide explains what you see, you'll come to a better understanding of this old subculture that still exists in New Orleans.

Voodoo is a combination of Catholicism and spiritual practices from the West African tribes. It was widely practiced during New Orleans' struggles with yellow fever and slavery, as well as it is today.

Ask about the voodo & cemetery tour, or the rituals. The Queen of Voodoo, Marie Laveau, is buried in the St. Louis Cemetery #1. The front shop sells voodoo dolls, gris-gris potions, and African masks.

Museum Hours - Daily 10am-8pm
Tours (Sunday 1 pm only) .. 10:30 am, 1 pm

Cost
Adults $6
College Students $5
High School Students $4
Elementary Students $3

Directions (in the French Quarter)
On Dumaine, between Royal and Bourbon Streets.

NEW ORLEANS PHARMACY MUSEUM

514 Chartres
504-565-8027

Visit an authentic apothecary, now a National Historic Landmark.

The first licensed pharmacist in America, Louis J. Dufilho, Jr., constructed an apothecary in the French Quarter in 1823. His handblown apothecary jars contained crude drugs, voodoo potions, powders, and medicinal herbs. Many of the medicinal herbs he needed grew out back in the courtyard.

Tour on your own. The Pharmacy Museum features rare patented medicines, medical instruments, Civil War surgical instruments, cosmetics, the old prescription files, and more.

The pharmacy contains an 1855 Italian-made soda fountain, with black and rose marble.

The museum offers guided museum and courtyard tours for groups of 10 or more. Call in advance.

Hours

Closed holidays

Tues.- Sun. .... 10 am - 5 pm

Cost

Adults $2
Seniors and Students 13 - 17 .... $1
Children under 12 .... Free

(Group rates available)

Directions

In the French Quarter on Chartres between Toulouse and St. Louis Streets.

OLD U.S. MINT

400 Esplanada Avenue
504-568-6968

An old U.S. Mint now houses Jazz artifacts

The Old U.S. Mint, built in 1835 during Andrew Jackson's presidency, supplied money for a rapidly developing country. Operations at the Old U.S. Mint continued until 1909. For a brief time (from 1861-1862), it stamped Confederate coins. Today, the Old U.S Mint is a part of the Louisiana State Museum.

The Old U.S. Mint now houses exhibits on Jazz Music. See the cornet that Louie Armstrong learned to play while living at the local boy's home in 1913. The music section features ragtime, early jazz, big bands, and modern jazz. Learn about New Orleans prodigies like Louis Armstrong, Jelly Roll Morton, Sidney Bechet, and Buddy Bolden. Or Blue Lu Barker, Sweet Emma Barrett, or Lizzie Miles.

Hours
Tues.- Sun. .... 9 am - 5 pm

Cost
Adults $5
Seniors and Students $4
Children under 12 .... Free

Direction
On Esplanada between Decatur and N. St. Peters Streets. Across from the French Market.

OLD URSULINE CONVENT
1116 Chartres Street
504-529-3040

Visit the beautiful old convent in the French Quarters

Built in 1734, the old Ursuline Convent, the oldest French Colonial building in the Mississippi Valley, survived the great fire of 1788. The fire destroyed the St. Louis Cathedral and over eight hundred homes, but it didn't burn the convent. It was saved because of a black bucket brigade.

Here's where the settlers' girls living in the French Quarter were educated during the 18th and 19th centuries. Established in 1727, the Ursuline Academy is considered the oldest girls' school in our country. The nuns at this convent, however, did establish a free school for black and Indian children.

Take the 45-minute tour of the formal gardens, the 1st floor of the convent, and St. Mary's Church. The church, owned by the Archdiocese of New Orleans, was built in 1845.

Tour Hours
Tues. - Fri. . . . 10 am, 11 am, 1 pm, 2 pm, 3 pm
Sat. - Sun. . . . . 11:15 am, 1 pm, 2 pm

Cost
Adults $5
Students $2
Children under 8 . . . . Free
Seniors $4

Directions
In the French Quarter on Chartres Street between Ursulines and Governor Nicholls Streets.

PITOT HOUSE MUSEUM

1440 Moss Street
504-482-0312

One of only a few old plantation homes still lining Bayou St. John

A New Orleans landmark, the Pitot House. Built in 1799, this old country plantation home once provided the aristocratic Bosque family a summer weekend retreat from the French Quarter. With large wide porches overlooking Bayou St. John, the house was meant to be shady and cool. Unique, it was built in a traditional West Indies style and is noted for its construction of posts and bricks covered with stucco.

Later in 1810, the house sold to James Pitot. While living here, he served from 1804-1805 as the first mayor of the newly incorporated New Orleans. In 1904, Mother Frances Xavier Cabrini bought the house for a convent. She was the first American citizen to be canonized as a saint by the Catholic Church. In 1962, the convent donated the manor to the Louisiana Landmarks Society. Moved a block from its original location, the house now sits on the site of the first French settlement in New Orleans in 1708.

Today, the house, completely restored and refurbished with Louisiana and American antiques from the 1800s, makes a favorite setting for weddings. Take the tour of the house and grounds.

Hours (Last tour at 2 pm)

Wed. - Sat. . . . . 10 am - 3 pm

Cost

Adults $5
Children under 12 . . . . $2
Seniors $4

Directions

On Moss Street on St. John's Bayou.

PRESBYTERE

710 Chartres
504-568-6968

Museum on Louisiana's cultural history

The Presbytere, part of the Louisiana State Museum, looks like the Cabildo. Both, along with the 1850 House, and the U.S. Mint are National Historic Landmarks. Originally built to house the monks of St. Louis Cathedral, the Presbytere now houses the exhibits *Marti Gras: It's Carival Time in Louisiana*.

The exhibits include two floors of history and artifacts pertaining to Carnival season.

Hours

Tues.- Sun. . . . . 9 am - 5 pm

Cost

Adults $5
Students with ID $4
Seniors $4
Children under 12 . . . . Free

Directions

In Jackson Square on Chartres Street at St. Peters Street in the French Quarter

ST. LOUIS CATHEDRAL

721 Chartres
504-525-9585

Walk inside the oldest church in the United States, the St. Louis Cathedral. Destroyed by a hurricane in 1722 and then later by fire in 1788, the cathedral you see today (built 1794) is the third on this site. It stands as New Orleans' most famous landmark. The city named the cathedral after the saint-king Louis IX of France, who led two crusades to the Holy Land. See him pictured in the huge mural behind the altar.

In 1964, Pope Paul VI designated the St. Louis Cathedral as a minor basilica. Later, in 1987, Pope John Paul II made a visit.

The cathedral faces the city's square—Jackson Square—with two Spanish Colonial-style buildings flanking either side. Looking directly at the cathedral, the one on the left, the Cabildo, once housed the Spanish government. The one on the right was intended to house monks. Both are part of the Louisiana State Museum.

Lining Jackson Square, the row houses (Pontalba Apartments) and shops are among the oldest in our country.

Take the 15-minute tour of the cathedral. Visit the gardens around back, where Creole gentlemen once dueled.

Tour Hours

Mon. - Sat. . . . . 9 am - 5 pm
Sunday . . . . 1:30 pm - 5 pm

Cost

Free

Directions

In the French Quarter in Jackson Square on Chartres St.

IN THE FRENCH QUARTER:

102 105 108 113 114 115

Chapter 4
NEW ORLEANS' THEATERS AND THE ARTS

A GALLERY OF FINE PHOTOGRAPHY

322 Royal Street
504-568-1313

A photo gallery with many rare and interesting photos

Into photography? You'll love seeing the two floors of framed photos in A Gallery of Fine Photography. Many rare. Their huge collection includes 19th- and 20th-century photos from around the world. See photos from famous photographers such as Ansel Adams, Elliott Erwitt, Jock Sturges, Henri Cartier-Bresson, Alfred Steigletz, O'Winston Link and over a hundred others.

Learn more about photography from its beginning in 1840 through contemporary times. Plan to spend an hour or two browsing through the gallery. Note the Herman Leonard jazz photos, the high point of their collection.

Hours

Mon. - Sat. . . . . 10 am - 6 pm
Sunday . . . . 11 am - 6 pm

Directions

On Royal at between Bienville and Conti Streets in the French Quarter.

CONTEMPORARY ARTS CENTER

900 Camp Street
504-523-1216 or 504-528-3800

Contemporary art center in New Orleans

Located inside an old restored warehouse, the Contemporary Arts Center anchors the Warehouse/Art District. It hosts concerts, films, theatrical and dance performances. With 10,000 square feet of gallery space, it offers a world of artistic ideas that's fun to explore. You'll notice that this old restored warehouse is a work of art, too. In fact, it's an award-winning building. See how well the old historic features mix with the contemporary. Plan to spend time browsing. The center's Cybercafe not only serves lunch, it has free Internet access. Buy tickets for any city event from the concierge.

Gallery Hours

Tues.-Sat. .... 10 am - 5 pm
Sunday .... 11 am - 5 pm

Cost

Members .... Free
Non-members $3
Seniors/Students $2
Thursdays .... Free

Directions

On Camp Street at Joseph Street
in the Warehouse/Art District.

JULIA STREET'S GALLERY ROW
Julia Street
New Orleans' Warehouse Art District

The K&B Corporation donated its former warehouse to a group of struggling artists who wanted to exhibit their work. That brought about the Contemporary Art Center. Since its opening in 1976, many art galleries have relocated to Warehouse/Art District. Nowadays, the area booms with emerging artists and affordable collectibles.

The first Saturday of each month, the galleries on Julia Street's Gallery Row create a festive atmosphere to show off their new exhibits. The first Saturday in October, the galleries in the district hold "Art for Art's Sake" on Julia Street. Thousands attend this event.

The following galleries you will find in the Warehouse/Art District. Most are located on Julia Street. Ask. Shops hand out maps to the area's galleries. Shop hours varies; some close Mondays. Most open 10 am - 5 pm. To get to Julia Street from the French Quarter, take St. Charles Avenue.

Ya\Ya Gallery	628 Baronne St.	504-529-3306
Estudio Gallery	630B Baronne St.	504-524-7982
Marguerite Oestreicher Fine Arts	626 Julia St.	504-581-9253
Galerie Simonne Stern	518 Julia St.	504-529-1118
New Orleans Auction Galleries	510 Julia St.	504-566-1849
Arthur Roger Gallery	432 Julia St.	504-522-1999
LeMieux Galleries	332 Julia St.	504-522-5988
Still-Zinsel Contemporary Fine Art	624 Julia St.	504-588-9999
Christopher Maier Furniture Design	329 Julia St.	504-586-9079

LE PETIT THEATER DU VIEUX CARRE

616 St. Peter Street
504-522-2081

Charming old historic theater in the French Quarter

Le Petit Theater's performing season begins in September and ends in June. That's been the norm for a long time. It's the oldest continuously operating community theater in our country.

Treat yourself to one of their fantastic performances. The theater offers 6 musicals and plays a year. Performances include Broadway favorites. They also do 4 children's productions annually. The theater's lovely courtyard with its tiered water fountain and lush vegetation makes intermission part of the delightful experience.

The theater also hosts events for the Tennessee Williams Festival in March.

Hours
Box Office
Mon. - Sat. 9 am - 5 pm

Cost
Musicals $20
Plays $18
Children's plays $7.50

Directions
On St. Peter St., between Chartres and Royal Streets in the French Quarter.

LOUISIANA PHILHARMONIC ORCHESTRA

305 Baronne St. Suite 600
504-523-6530 ex. 237

New Orleans' fine philharmonic orchestra

The Louisiana Philharmonic Orchestra's performing season of classical works takes place in the Orpheum Theater at 129 University Place. In addition to their regular performing season, the orchestra puts on a Classic Series at the Pontchartrain Center at 4545 Williams Boulevard. The orchestra's known for its rich history of performing classical music. Call for a schedule of their upcoming performances or call Ticketmasters, 504-522-5555.

In October on a Sunday afternoon, the orchestra performs under the magnificent 300-year-old oak trees at Oak Alley Plantation. Attendees soak up the beautiful surroundings while eating their picnic lunches. Mark your calendar for this event.

Hours
Box Office
Mon. - Fri. . . . . 9 am - 5 pm

Cost
Tickets . . . . $11 - $52

Directions
At Baronne Street at Gravier Street above
O'Henry's Food & Spirits.

MAGAZINE STREET GALLERIES

800-387-8924
www.magazinestreet.com

Funky, fun collectibles

It's necessary to know that Magazine Street runs from the French Quarter (Canal Street) all the way to the Audubon Zoo, 6 miles. Because of the distance, it's best to go by car. On the way, you'll find 15 art galleries with a diversity of artwork and prices much more affordable then on Royal Street. Shops offer one-of-kind pottery, furniture, jewelry, photography, books, regional art pieces, and other specialties. Most shops open from 10 am - 5 pm, Monday - Saturday. Some close on Mondays.

Alex And Cindy Williams' Potsalot
	2029 Magazine St.	(504) 524-6238
Artifacts (Fine Craft Gallery)	5515 Magazine St.	(504) 899-5505

Berta's and Mina's Antiquities - NL Folk Art Gallery
	4138 Magazine St.	(504) 895-6201
Casey Willems Pottery	3919 Magazine St.	(504) 899-1174
Cole Pratt Gallery	3800 Magazine St.	(504) 891-6789
Contemporary Arts Center	900 Camp St.	(504) 528-3800
Davis Gallery	3964 Magazine St.	(504) 897-0780
Diva Gallery/Studio	1110 Antonine St.	(504) 899-0275

Dominique Giordano Design (Next to BP Station)
	5420 Magazine St.	(504) 895-3909
Morgan West Studio/Gallery	3326 Magazine St.	(504) 895-7976

New Orleans Academy of Fine Arts/Academy Gallery
	5256 Magazine St.	(504) 899-8111

The New Orleans School of Glassworks and Printmaking Studio
	727 Magazine St.	(504) 529-7277
Reina Gallery	4132 Magazine St.	(504) 895-0022
Shadyside Pottery Shop	3823 Magazine St.	(504) 897-1710
The Westgate	5219 Magazine St.	(504) 899-3077
Wyndy Morehead Fine Arts	3926 Magazine St.	(504) 269-8333

MUSIC VENUES

New Orleans Music

New Orleans is best known for jazz—thanks to early musicians (Louis Armstrong, Buddy Bolden, King Oliver, and Jelly Roll Morton.) **Traditional jazz** still thrives at places like Preservation Hall and Palm Court Café (Percy Humphrey, Pud Brown, and Wendell Brunious). Some of the finest **modern jazz** musicians (Red Tyler, Tony Dagradi, and Peter Martin) and **avant garde jazz** artists (Alvin Batiste, Earl Turbinton, and Edward Jordan) you'll find at Snug Harbor or Café Brazil. **Rhythm and Blues, gospel, Latin, zydeco,** and **Cajun** music contribute to New Orleans' fine music scene.

In and Around the French Quarter

Donna's Bar and Grill	800 N. Rampart (at St. Ann)
	504-895-8081 Brass bands
Funky Butt	714 N. Rampart (btwn Orleans and St. Ann)
	504-558-0872 Modern jazz
House of Blues	225 Decatur St. (between Iberville and Bienville)
	504-529-2624 Rock, alternative rock,
	R&B, blues, zydeco, contemporary jazz,
	funk, gospel
Palm Court Café	1204 Decatur St. (between Governor Nicholls and Barracks)
	504-525-0200 Traditional jazz
Preservation Hall	726 St. Peters (between Royal and Bourbon)
	504-522-2841 Traditional jazz
Tip's French Quarter	233 N. Peters 504-566-7095
Storyville District	125 Bourbon 504-410-1000 (at Iberville)
	Traditional and modern jazz, blues

Uptown

Tipitina's 501 Napoleon Avenue (at Tchoupitoulas St.)
504-895-8477 (Home of the late Professor Longhair and the Neville Brothers) Rock, alternative rock, New Orleans funk, gospel, zydeco, blues, contemporary jazz, Cajun

Snug Harbor 626 Frenchman St. (between Royal and Chartres) 504-949-0696 Contemporary jazz, R&B

Faubourg Marigny

Café Brazil 2100 Chartres St. (at Frenchman Sts.) 504-949-0851 Jazz, R&B, zydeco, Latin, reggae

The Dragon's Den 435 Esplanade Avenue 504-949-1750 (at Decatur) Rock, blues, Cajun

Warehouse Arts and Mid-City Districts

Howlin Wolf 828 S. Peters (between Julia and St. Joseph) 504-523-2551 Contemporary rock

Mid-City Lane Rock 'n Bowl 4133 S. Carrollton Ave. (Tulane and Canal) 504-482-3133 R&B, zydeco, rockabilly, blues

The Praline Connection Gospel and Blues Hall   907 S. Peters St. (between Joseph and North Diamond Sts.) 504-523-3973

NEW ORLEANS BALLET ASSOCIATION

305 Baronne Street Suite 700
504-522-0996

Ballet at its finest—in New Orleans

The New Orleans Ballet offers wonderful performances in the Mahalia Jackson Theater of the Performing Arts in Armstrong Park at Basin Street. As a service, the association invites dance companies from around the world to perform; it doesn't have its own dance company. Their season runs from October through May and includes 7 to 8 performances a year. Season tickets are available. The Ballet offers special matinee performances and dance classes for children. Last minute tickets, if available, are   price for students. Call for their performing schedule or call Ticketmaster at 504-522-5555.

Hours

Mon. - Fri. . . . . 9 am - 5 pm

Cost (tickets)

Adults . . . . $22 - 66
Senior/Students . . . . $7 off

Directions

At Baronne Street at Gravier Street above
O'Henry's Food & Spirits.

NEW ORLEANS OPERA ASSOCIATION
305 Baronne Street 5th floor
504-529-2278

Oldest opera company in America

If you're into opera, call for a listing of the New Orleans Opera Association's upcoming productions. Each year the association produces four operas: October, November, December, and March. Season tickets available. Performances take place at the Mahalia Jackson Theater of the Performing Arts in Armstrong Park at Basin Street. For good seating, call well in advance. Best seats: orchestra parquet. The new annual holiday production of *Cinderella* is ideal for a great family Christmas tradition. Call for their schedule or call Ticketmaster, 504-522-5555.

The first opera on the North American continent was staged in New Orleans May 21, 1796. The New Orleans Opera Association has produced operas for over 50 years. They are part of the longest consecutively running opera company in America.

Hours
Box Office
Mon. - Fri. .... 10 am - 5 pm

Cost
Ticket $20-90

Directions
At Baronne Street at Gravier Street above O'Henry's Food & Spirits.

OUTDOOR SCULPTURE GARDENS AND ARTWORK

Hotel Inter-Continental New Orleans

444 St. Charles Avenue • 504-525-5566

See the artwork in this grand hotel

Located only a few blocks from the galleries in the Warehouse/Art District, this swanky hotel's lobby glows with fine pieces of New Orleans' contemporary art. Once you've seen the lobby, head for the fifth-floor courtyard for more. The courtyard is elegantly landscaped with fine sculptures, all done by locals, too. You'll find the hotel on St. Charles Avenue, between Poydras and Gravier Streets.

K&B Plaza

1055 St. Charles Avenue • 504-586-1234

If art is exciting, you'll enjoy seeing the sculpture gallery in K&B Plaza on St. Charles Avenue at Lee Circle. Enjoy seeing a collection of impressive 20th-century contemporary artwork.

Woldenberg Riverfront Park

Woldenberg Riverfront Park is also an important stop for art lovers. The outdoor sculpture garden features major artworks of well-known artists.

SAENGER PERFORMING ARTS CENTER

143 N. Rampart St.
504-524-2490

Take in a Broadway show or a rock concert

This majestic old movie palace hosts traveling Broadway shows. Recently touring productions include *Footloose*, *Tony and Tina's Wedding*, *Cabaret*, and *River Dance*. The annual season features 5 to 7 shows from musicals to variety shows. Pop and rock stars perform here, too.

The Italian baroque interior will make an impression. The ceiling is beautiful, with stars twinkling in a night sky and Greek statues framing the top balcony. Observe the pipe organ. It's the largest the Robert Morton Company has ever made and the chandelier in the lobby once hung in the palace of Versailles, France. The theater is listed on the National Register of Historic Places.

Hours

Box Office

Mon. - Fri. . . . . 10 am - 5 pm

Cost

Tickets vary according to show

Directions

On N. Rampart Street, between Canal and Iberville Streets.

SOUTHERN REP THEATRE

Canal Place Shopping Center
200 Canal Street
504-861-8163

Local playwrights' productions

This intimate theater seats only 150, so don't hesitate to get reservations. Devoted to southern playwrights, the theater produces plays by well-known and emerging authors. See favorites by Tennessee Williams, who once lived in New Orleans. The annual season runs from September to June. Call the box office for their upcoming schedule. The box office is at 501 Pine Street.

Hours
Box Office
Mon. - Fri. 1 pm - 5 pm

Cost
All shows . . . . $20 per person

Directions
The theater is in the Canal Place Shopping Center on the third floor.

STORYVILLE DISTRICT

125 Bourbon Street
504-410-1000

New Orleans' jazz and tasty food

New. Storyville District intends to promote New Orleans' jazz in the best way possible—great musicians, great food, in a terrific place. The famous restaurant owner Ralph Brennan and producer Quint Davis of the New Orleans Jazz & Heritage Festival opened Storyville as a joint venture. With no cover charge except during Mardi Gras, the Jazz Fest, and the French Quarter Festival, feel free to walk in, wander around, order an appetizer, or eat dinner while listening to famous jazz combos. Sundays include a buffet.

Hours

Daily . . . . 2:30 pm - closing time varies
(Midnight - 1:30 am)

Cost

Appetizers $3-7
Entrees . . . . $11 - 17

Directions

On Bourbon Street at Iberville Street.

UNIVERSITY OF NEW ORLEANS THEATRE

Elysian Fields Avenue
504-280-6381(Box office)

Nationally recognized university theater

Enjoy entertaining live drama at bargain prices at the University of New Orleans Theatre. Student productions include classics, musicals, plays by student playwrights, and winners of the Tennessee Williams One-Act Playwright Competition. See productions such as Shakespeare's *The Merchant of Venice* and Mozart's *The Magic Flute,* offering about six shows a year. Season ticket holders save even more ($25 general; $16 student). Call to reserve a seat. All performances are held in the Performing Arts Center on the Lakefront Campus. Theater opens 1 hour before curtain time.

Hours

Box Office (opens the Monday of a each new show)

Mon. - Fri.	10 am - 3 pm
Performances	8 pm
Matinees	2:30 pm

Cost

Adults	$8
Seniors/Students	$5
Children under 12	$5

Directions

Take Elysian Fields Avenue north of I-10 to Leon C. Simon Street and go left. Turn right on St. Anthony and watch for the Perfoming Arts Center and box office.

WYLAND WALL

New Orleans Hilton Riverside Hotel
2 Poydras Street
504-529=2865
www.wyland.com

New Orleans' "Whaling Wall"

The artist Wyland's mission is clear: "We must preserve the environment before it's too late." He tirelessly expresses that message every time he paints one of his "Whaling Wall" murals. He intends to paint 100 walls before 2011. So far he has completed 78.

You'll find his 69th "Whaling Wall" on the side of the Hilton Riverside Hotel, in front of the parking lot. He painted it as a gift to the city of New Orleans during the 1997 Jazz and Heritage Festival. It was also the International Year of the Ocean. Titled "Blue Whales," the mural stands 66-feet tall and 250-feet long.

Look for the mural from the Crescent City Bridge. Be sure to take time to see it up close.

Currently, Wyland hosts his second season of his underwater television series on the Discovery Channel. The program's known as "Wyland's Ocean World." Chosen as the Official Marine Artist of the Millennium by Disney, Wyland is now creating a sculpture of sea animals for the Epcot Center at Disney World.

Directions

On Convention Center Blvd. at Girod Street.

IN THE FRENCH QUARTER:
126 121 124 132 134 136

Chapter 5
AMUSEMENT PARKS, ATTRACTIONS & TOURS

CAROLYN KOLB'S FILM SITE TOURS
504-861-8158

Many a movie was filmed in the French Quarter

Any movie buff will find this tour interesting. It lasts about 90 minutes and takes you on a 25-block stroll to places you'll recognize seeing in movies. You'll be amazed at the number of times you've seen the French Quarter on the big screen. Movies include *Interview with a Vampire, Angel Heart, Walk on the Wild Side, Panic in the Streets,* and many others. Schedule your tour. If you have a particular interest, let them know and they'll be glad to include that in the tour, too.

Hours
Call for an appointment and the meeting place

Cost
Per person $20

CARRIAGE RIDES
Decatur Street at Jackson Square

Step back into New Orleans' past

See the French Quarter from an old-fashioned mule-drawn carriage. While you're slowly moving about holding up traffic, your friendly driver gives you a history of the French Quarter. Don't take every thing he tells you to heart—it's probably not all that accurate. Carriages carry up to six and cost the same if it's for one or six. If you call Good Old Day Carriages (540-523-0804), a carriage will pick you up in front of your French Quarter or Business District hotel. Enjoy a ride one evening after dinner.

Carriages are available except between 4 pm - 5 pm
when mules and drivers change.

Hours
Daily .... 9 am - 10 pm

Cost
Half hour $55
One hour $105

Directions
In the French Quarter, on Decatur
in front of Jackson Square.

CRADLE OF JAZZ TOURS
504-282-3583

New Orleans' jazz heritage

If you're a music lover, this tour will be important. From an air-conditioned van, visit landmarks and peek at early pioneer jazz musicians' homes while listening to their music. John McCusker, a news photographer, has spent years researching the city's jazz heritage. The tour lasts 3 hours and includes a take-home photograph booklet.

Call for a reservation. The van will pick you up at your hotel.

Hours
Saturdays . . . . 10 am

Cost
Adults $25
Children under 12 . . . . Free

Directions
The van will come to your hotel.

ENTERGY IMAX THEATER

I Canal Street
504- 581-4629 or 800-774-7394

See the world without leaving New Orleans

Named after the company that made it possible, the Entergy IMAX Theater has a screen that's 5½ stories tall and a 12,500-watt digital sound system. Climb Everest. Explore the Grand Canyon or fly with the Blue Angels. Orbit in space as if you were there. New films always coming. Shows last about 40 minutes. Best of all, get one of the four different discount combination tickets and enjoy the other attractions: Aquariums of the Americas, the Audubon Zoo, and the John James Audubon Riverboat Shuttle, too. Prices vary depending on the combination.

Hours for shows

Shows begin every hour on the hour, call ahead for shows playing
Daily ('til 8 pm in the summer) .... 10 am - 6 pm

Cost

Adults $7.75
Children 2 - 12 .... $5
Seniors $6.75

Directions

On the riverfront, adjacent to the
Aquarium of the Americas.

FRIENDS OF THE CALIDO-FRENCH QUARTER WALKING TOUR
504-523-3939

Walk the French Quarter with a local historian

Meet at 523 St. Ann Street (at 1:30 pm) any day of the week for a historic tour of the French Quarter. Reservations aren't required. A ticket for the tour also gives you admission to two other Louisiana State Museum attractions: the 1850 House and Madame John's Legacy (plus 15% discount at the gift shop).

The tour lasts approximately 2 hours and is one of the best ways to get a historic overview of the French Quarter, featuring its history, architecture, and folklore. See a copy of the 1803 Louisiana Purchase.

Hours for tours

Monday .... 1:30 pm
Tues. - Sun. .... 10 am - 1:30 pm

Cost

Adults $10
Children under 12 .... Free
Seniors/Students $8

Directions

Meet at 523 St. Ann Street,
between Decatur and Chartres Streets.

GARDEN DISTRICT AND LAFAYETTE CEMETERY TOUR

Restless Spirit Tours
Igor's Lounge
2133 St. Charles Avenue
504-895-0895

Visit the Lafayette Cemetery #1. This old cemetery dates back to 1833 and has long interested visitors to New Orleans. It was Mark Twain who called them "Cities of the Dead" because the vaults sit above ground.

Then see the homes of such notables as author Anne Rice, football player Archie Manning, and recording artist Trent Reznor. Your guide will tell you about the history and architecture of the largest collection of antebellum mansions in the United States. Considered an architectural melting pot, see examples of Greek Revival, Gothic, Corinthian, Ionic, and Victorian styles. Tour lasts 2½ hours.

Hours

Daily . . . . 10:30 am & 1:30 pm

Cost

Adults $13
Seniors/Students $11
Children 12 and under $6

Directions

Meet at Igor's Lounge. Take St. Charles Streetcar to Jackson Avenue.

JAZZLAND THEME PARK

12301 Lake Forest Boulevard
504-242-2324 (Administration)

New Orleans' awesome new theme park

(New Orleans' new theme park opens May 2000.)

Jazzland features one of the largest steel roller coasters in the country, standing 12 stories tall and 3400 feet long with eight different twists. This park's 31 rides compete with those in Texas and Alabama. Enjoy an airboat journey, a simulated rocket ride, and an extra-thrilling log ride.

Live musical entertainment, alligator wrestlers, a Mardi Gras parade, and restaurants that showcase Louisiana culture. The 7 theme areas include the Kids' Section.

Hours & Cost

Call for this information when park's about to open

Directions

At the intersection of I-10 and I-510 in New Orleans, 12 miles from downtown.

LAKE LAWN METAIRIE CEMETERY

5100 Pontchartrain Boulevard
504-486-6331

Visit one of New Orleans old historic cemeteries

A trip to a New Orleans cemetery ought to be one of your stops. But it's not wise to wander through one of these "Cities of the Dead" alone. Lake Lawn Metairie Cemetery, one of the safest, allows you to enjoy the experience from your car. Hand your driver's license to one of the florists at the flower shop near the cemetery's entrance. In return, you'll receive a tape recorder and tape along with a map for a 40-minute self-guided tour.

Pick a recording that interests you. You'll listen to some incredible stories and see some remarkable monuments. Some are in the shapes of miniature temples, pyramids, mosques, and pagodas. In fact, you'll see the all kinds of architecture. New Orleans sits below sea level, so all the monuments are above ground. The cemetery is listed on the National Registry of Historic Places.

Of the 42 cemeteries in the New Orleans area, Lake Lawn Metairie is considered the most beautiful and the most unique.

Hours

Daily including holidays . . . 8:30 am - 3:30 pm

Cost

Free

Directions

The cemetery is located on Pontchartrain Boulevard at Meatier Road in the Mid City District.

LOUISIANA SUPERDOME TOUR
1500 Sugar Bowl Drive
504-587-3808

Largest indoor arena in the world

You'll be impressed with the Louisiana Superdome's magnitude. It stands 27 stories high and covers 52 acres. The Superdome seats a large number of people: 70,000 for football and 87,500 for concerts. The tour takes about an hour and varies according to their event schedule. Watch a 15-minute video; visit the locker rooms, the media area, the upper levels, and the luxury box suites.

Buy your tickets at the ticket office located at Gate A on Poydras Street. Parking is available at the VIP parking lot to the right of the ticket office. Remember to bring your parking ticket to the ticket office for validation. Groups of 15 or more must call ahead.

Hours
Weekdays ..... 10:30 am, Noon, and 1:30 pm

Cost
Adults $6
Children 5 - 10 .... $4
Seniors 62+ $5

Directions
On Poydras Street at LaSalle Street.

MID-CITY LANES ROCK 'N' BOWL

4133 S. Carrollton Avenue
504-482-3133

Top musicians perform in bowling alley

Don't let the appearance of this place stop you from experiencing one of the hottest music venues in New Orleans. Located in an old bowling alley. The locals pack the place the nights popular local bands play. Listen to these fine musicians perform while bowling, or eating at the snack bar that serves fried alligator, gumbo, po-boys and the like.

Two stages on either side of a dance floor offer non-stop music. Dance away or watch from seats along the sides. Bands known to play here include Boozoo Chavis, The Iguanas, Nathan and the Zydeco Cha Chas. No bands on Sundays and Mondays. The bands playing determine the closing time. Call before going. Come early if you want a seat. Experience a part of New Orleans where tourists don't generally go.

Hours

Mon. - Thurs. . . . . Opens at 4 pm
Fri., Sat., & Sun. . . . . Opens at Noon

Cost

Depends on the band playing
$5-10
Bowling $10/hour

Directions

From the French Quarter take Canal Street
to Carrollton Avenue. Go left 6 blocks.
Will be on the right at Tulane Street.

NEW ORLEANS FAIR GROUNDS
1751 Gentilly Boulevard
504-944-5515 • www.fgno.com

Thoroughbred racing at this historic racetrack

A new, six-level, 217,000 square-foot grandstand now stands where the historic one burned down in 1993. Looking very much like the old one, the new facility offers lots of modern conveniences and amenities.

The New Orleans Fair Grounds is the third oldest racetrack in the country. Big races take place here, the New Orleans Handicap (for older horses) and the Louisiana Derby (for 3-year-olds). This is a major race leading up the Kentucky Derby. Both are held in March. The racetrack runs Thanksgiving Day through March. Call for a reservation at the Clubhouse Dining Room, 504-943-2200 or 800-262-7983.

During each racing season the Fair Grounds host a Family Day. Much like a mini-carnival out on the racetrack, activities include puppet shows, face painters, pony rides, carousel rides, refreshments, and more. All activities are free. Call for date and time.

The racetrack's name came about because the Mechanics and Agricultural Association once held their fair here. These days it is the site for the New Orleans Jazz and Heritage Festival the last weekend in April and the first weekend in May.

Hours
Seasonal opening Thanksgiving Day

Cost
Grandstand $1
Clubhouse $4

Directions
Mid-City District, 10 minutes from the French Quarter. From the French Quarter, take Esplanade Ave. northwest to Gentilly Blvd going northeast. Will be on the left.

NEW ORLEANS SCHOOL OF GLASS WORKS AND PRINTMAKING STUDIO

727 Magazine Street
504-529-7277

All you would like to know about the art of glass making

Stop in at the New Orleans School of Glass Works and Printmaking Studio and browse through their large gallery of fine glassware. Watch free daily demonstrations of the master craftsmen at work in front of huge state-of-the-art furnaces. This is the South's largest hot glass sculpture, printmaking, and bookbinding facility. You'll find this impressive.

Works displayed in the gallery are those of professional craftsmen on staff at the studio, some nationally known.

Ask about making a glass sculpture of your hand casting. It's by appointment only. It takes 30 minutes to cast your hand in sand and 3 days for the finished piece to be picked up or mailed. Lots of fun.

Ask about bronze pouring and sugar blowing, two new fun things you'll enjoy doing at this fascinating place. Note: The gallery closes on Saturdays during the hot summer months.

Hours for gallery

Mon. - Fri. (Summer) . . . . 11 am - 5 pm
Mon. - Sat. (Winter) . . . . 11 am - 5 pm

Cost

Free

Directions

On Magazine Street at Girod and Julia Street.

RIVERFRONT STREETCAR

Regional Transit Authorities
101 Dauphine Street 4th floor
504-242-2600 or 504-248-3900

Ride the along the riverfront on the streetcar

Ride along the riverfront in a shiny red streetcar. It travels past the French Quarter to the Warehouse/ Art District for 1.9 miles before returning. Enjoy the newly renovated riverfront area as the streetcar stops at attractions along the way.

A recent $14 million expansion project has now joined the Riverfront Streetcar line with the St. Charles line and a third line that runs along Canal Street. The Canal Street line will extend to the New Orleans Museum of Art in City Park sometime in the future. Visitors' passes are available for $4 a day or $8 for three consecutive days and allow unlimited travel on any public transportation, including buses. Ask for more information at your hotel or call the RTA.

Hours

Mon. - Fri. . . . . 6 am - 11:30 pm
Sat. and Sun. . . . . 8 am - 11:30 pm

Cost

Riverfront Streetcar
One way   (exact change required) . . $1.25
Canal Streetcar   (One way) $1

RIVERTOWN, USA

405 Williams Boulevard
Kenner, LA 70062
504-468-7231

A statue marks the spot where the explorer LaSalle stepped onto land from the Mississippi River in 1682 in the historic town of Kenner-Rivertown, USA. Besides the beautiful view of the river at LaSalle's Landing, Williams Boulevard offers several small, unpretentious museums of interest to children. The hours (Tuesday - Saturday, 9 am to 5 pm) and the admission ($3 for each museum) are the same; discount passes can be purchased for $10. The discount pass doesn't include the Children's Castle. Located 1/2 mile from the New Orleans International Airport. From downtown New Orleans, take I-10 west to Williams Boulevard. Go south towards the river. Once you've crossed the railroad tracks, you're in Rivertown.

Saints Hall of Fame
409 Williams Blvd. 504-468-6617

Mardi Gras Museum
407 Williams Blvd. 504-468-7258

Louisiana Toy Train Museum
519 Williams Blvd. 504-468-7223

Children's Castle
503 Williams Blvd. 504-468-7231

Daily Living Science Center
409A Williams Blvd. 504-468-7229

Louisiana Wildlife and Fisheries Museum
303 Williams Blvd. 504-468-7232

SAVE OUR CEMETERIES TOURS
305 Barrone Street #306 • 504-525-3377

Tour either of these historic old cemeteries

Admission for these tours helps preserve these old cemeteries. For a tour of the St. Louis Cemetery #1 located on Basin and St. Louis Streets, call for a reservation. After calling them, meet at 10 am at the Royal Blend Coffee Shop at 621 Royal Street. (This tour includes a security guard since it's one of the more dangerous cemeteries.)

A tour for the Lafayette Cemetery doesn't require a reservation and is located in the lovely Garden District. Simply meet Mondays, Wednesdays, Fridays, or Saturdays at 10:30 am at the (1400 block) Washington Avenue gate entrance for a tour of the Lafayette Cemetery #1. The tours give a history of the cemetery and the tombs. Both are very interesting.

Office Hours
Mon. - Fri. . . . . 9 am - 5 pm

Tour
Sunday . . . St Louis: 10 am . . Lafayette: 10:30 am

Cost
St. Louis Cemetery #1
Adults $12
Seniors $10
Children 12 - 18 . . . . $6

Lafayette Cemetery #1
Adults $6
Seniors/Students 12 - 18 . . . . $5
Children under 12 . . . . Free

Directions: Meet at the Royal Blend Coffee Shop at 623 Royal Street, between St. Peter and Toulouse Streets.

STORYLAND

City Park
Victory Avenue
504-483-9381 or 504-482-4888

Named one of the top ten playgrounds in the country by *Child* magazine

Kids will find Storyland fascinating. Located inside City Park, this fairy tale theme park's a winner. One of New Orleans' finest Mardi Gras float makers, Blaine Kern, Jr., created the sculpted characters for the larger-than-life storybook exhibits. Story boxes throughout the park recount fairy tales.

Children can climb into the mouth of Pinocchio's whale, fish in the Little Mermaid's Pond, and crawl up Miss Muffet's Spider Web. Regularly, local actors put on puppet shows at the Puppet Castle. A favorite place for birthday parties; call 504-488-2896 for details.

Hours

Seasonal, call for times

Cost

Per person $2
Children 2 and under . . . . Free

Directions

In City next to the Carousel Gardens on Victory Avenue.

VAMPIRE STREET THEATRE (RESTLESS SPIRIT TOURS)

Lafitte's Blacksmith Shop
941 Bourbon Street
504-895-0895

New Orleans' original vampire tour

The French Quarter's streets become the stage for this theatrical walking tour.

Guided by a master storyteller, this vampire tour capitalizes on New Orleans' dark side.

You'll hear tales of horror and of the living dead. Visit movie sites from Anne Rice's *Interview with a Vampire* and locations in her books. Creating national attention, this 2-hour tour has been featured in network documentaries.

Hours

Nightly .... 8:30 pm

Cost

Adults $13
Seniors/Students $11
Children 12 - 6 .... $6

Directions

On Bourbon Street at the corner of St. Philip Street.

WORLD TRADE CENTER
2 Canal Street
504-581-4888

River front high-rise with public observation deck

It takes 90 minutes to make a full revolution on the 33rd floor in the cocktail lounge known as the Top of the Mart. Leisurely enjoy a great view of the city's rooftops and the river. One of the best times to go is at sunset. Popular with tourists.

The World Trade Center houses many consulates and foreign agencies. You'll see the flags representing the countries on the ground floor. Be sure to visit the art exhibit (changing every two weeks) in the lobby. Note the Spanish plaza outside the building.

Hours

Mon-Fri. . . . . 10 am -11 pm
Saturday . . . . 11 am - 1 am
Sunday . . . . 2 pm - Midnight

Cost

Free
(Purchase of drink required.
Nonalcoholic drinks and snacks available.)
No children under 18 allowed.

Directions

On Canal Street at the river next
to the Convention Center.

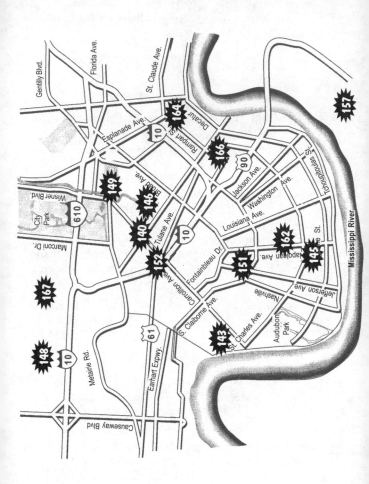

IN THE FRENCH QUARTER:
141 142 144 147 150 153 154 155
156 158 159 160 161 163 165

Chapter 6
EATING OUT IN NEW ORLEANS

ANGELO BROCATO

214 North Carrollton Avenue
504-486-0078

Sweets

All that's needed is Mickey Rooney and Judy Garland and this place would look like any malt shop from the 1940's. The difference is Brocato's serves Italian cookies, pastries, and ice cream. Special ice cream flavors imported from Italy include chestnut, Amaretto, and hazelnut. Cannoli, Italian seed cookies, biscotti, and Italian ice in flavors from mango to chocolate are all in the house. Try the spumoni, layered with three ice creams, pistachio, tuttifrutti, and lemon. It's an ice cream parlor . . . No, it's a bakery. It's bellisimo.

Hours

Sunday through Thursday . . . 9:30 am - 10 pm
Friday and Sat. . . . . until 10:30 pm

Cost

Moderate, varies

Directions

From downtown, take Canal Street to Carrollton Avenue.
Turn right, go one and a half blocks.

BAYONA

430 Dauphine St.
504-525-4455

"New World"

That's how renowned chef Susan Spicer labels her cuisine in this 19th-century French Quarter Creole cottage. The sweetbreads appetizer is one of the finest dishes in the city. Best bet: Grilled duck with pepper jelly glaze. A typical evening finds the place filled with local families, convention groups, and tourists because there's something for everybody, like the apple almond gratin with spice ice cream. Sit outside on the patio in cool months, sip cool drinks, and listen to the horse drawn carts clip clop by, because Bayona specializes in perfect evenings.

Hours

Lunch:
Monday - Friday .... 11:30 am - 1:30 pm
Dinner:
Monday - Thursday .... 6 pm - 9:30
Friday & Saturday .... until 10:30

Cost

Lunch entrees: $8 - $13
Dinner entrees: $14 -$21

Directions

Dauphine St. between St. Louis and Conti Streets,
French Quarter.

BELLA LUNA
914 North Peters
504-529-1583

Eclectic

Even if the food was not as incredible as it is, a trip to Bella Luna would be worthwhile for the magnificent, sweeping view of the Mississippi River and the French Quarter. Bright and airy in daylight, the restaurant is more dramatic at sunset. This elegant, contemporary French Market spot features oversize windows to watch the ships go by as you dine on expertly prepared osso bucco, veal T-bones with herb-infused olive oil or perfect pasta. The menu is continually evolving and always imaginative. Great spot for marriage proposals or family outings. Best bet: Save room for fudge brownie cappuccino pie.

Hours
Brunch
Sunday . . . . 11 am - 3 pm
Dinner
Monday - Saturday . . . . 6 pm - 10 pm

Cost
Entrees: $14 - $25

Location
Just across the street from the French Market
in the French Quarter.

BRIGTSEN'S

723 Dante Street
504-861-7610

Creole/Acadian

The setting is a 150-year-old uptown New Orleans house, artfully converted into an intimate, homey dining space much beloved among locals. The menu changes seasonally, but typical are tournedos of beef with Port and bleu cheese, or blackened prime rib. It's worth the trip for the mouth-watering sauces and the banana bread pudding and double chocolate cake. Brigtsen's has the feel of a lovely guest house on a quiet old New Orleans street. Ask for a table in the front sunroom.

Hours

Tuesday - Saturday . . . . 5:30 - 10pm

Cost

Entrees . . . . $10 - $22

Direction

Take historic St. Charles Avenue all the way uptown to Carrolton. Turn right, two blocks to Maple. Turn left, go two blocks to Dante and turn left. Second house on the left.

BROUSSARD'S

819 Conti St.
504-581-3866

Creole and Continental

A vintage New Orleans dining establishment, dating
to 1920 and serving all the dishes one expects from
a grand old Crescent City establishment. Three
luxurious dining rooms surround a lush French
Quarter courtyard. Try the shrimp and crab
cheesecake with roasted red pepper and dill cream.
Move on to the perfectly prepared rack of lamb or
pecan stuffed salmon. Desserts are as grand as the
atmosphere and worth saving room for. Best bet:
Crepes Broussard.

Hours

Nightly .... 6 - 10 pm

Cost

Entrees .... $17 - $26

Directions

Between Dauphine and Bourbon Streets, French Quarter.

CAFE ATCHAFALAYA

901 Louisiana Avenue
504-891-5271

Southern Home Cookin'

Start with fried green tomatoes or fried chicken livers with pepper jelly. Owner Iler Pope likes to call her creations "Rather Southern—Slightly Sophisticated." This is the place to go for down-home cookin', like chicken and dumplings, country fried steak with creamy gravy, stuffed pork chops and cornbread dressing. The perfect accompaniment to all of it? Pope's secret recipe jalapeno cheese bread. It's addictive. Best bet: For breakfast on weekends, try the praline waffles or grillades and jalapeno grits. You're going to ooh and ah at the first bite.

Hours

Lunch: Tuesday - Sunday . . . . 11:30 am - 2 pm
Dinner : Tuesday - Thursday . . . . . . 5:30 - 9 pm
Friday and Saturday . . . . to 10 pm
Breakfast: Saturday and Sunday 8:30 am - 2 pm

Cost

Lunch . . . . $5.95 - $13.95
Dinner . . . . $5.95 - $19.95

Directions

From downtown, take historic St. Charles Avenue to Louisiana Avenue. Turn left and go to the 900 block.

CHRISTIAN'S

3835 Iberville Street
504-482-4924

French Creole

Christian's has the distinction of being the only restaurant in town located in an old church. High vaulted ceilings and beautiful stained glass windows are intact, as is the altar, which is now the waiter's station. One bite of fried oysters wrapped in bacon and topped with meuniere sauce will cause you to praise the cook and bless the palate. At lunch try the eggplant stuffed with shrimp and crabmeat and for dinner (because you will be back) do not miss Shrimp Marigny, flamed in brandy. Not sure what's cooking? Check the sermon board out front.

Hours

Lunch:
Tuesday - Friday . . . . 11:30 - 2 pm
Dinner:
Tuesday - Saturday . . . . 5:30 pm - 9:30 pm

Cost

Lunch entrees: $12.50 -$ 21.00
Dinner entrees: $17.00 - $28.25

Directions

From downtown take Canal Street to the 3800 block. Take a right on North Scott Street. Go one block until you see the church.

CROISSANT D'OR

617 Ursuline Street
504-524-4663

Pastries

What once was an Italian ice cream parlor (and still looks like one) is now a distinctively European pastry shop, complete with a lovely courtyard and a bubbling fountain. Shop the colorful, well-stocked pastry cases and enjoy your selections (all baked that morning on premises) with a hearty, oversize cup of New Orleans coffee. Great Sunday morning suggestion: Take a leisurely stroll through the French Quarter to Croissant d'Or for breakfast, and then continue on to the flea market in the French Market. Move on to the nearby moonwalk and stroll along the Mississippi. After all, it's Sunday.

Hours

Daily . . . . 7 am - 5 pm

Cost

Varies, but a great breakfast can be had for well under $10

Directions

Ursuline Street, between Royal and Chartres Streets, French Quarter.

FOODIE'S KITCHEN

720 Veterans Blvd.
Metairie, LA
504-837-9695

A little of everything!

The newest concept by the owners of Commander's Palace is billed as a gourmet meals market, where you can dine in or carry out a multi-course meal for guests, complete with a bouquet of flowers, freshly baked bread, wine, hors d'oeuvres, salads, entrees, and irresistible desserts. Hot items like crawfish étoufée or deli counter offerings, including everything from fresh pasta to spicy Creole chicken salad to extra thick pork chops and fresh seafood. Oh, and what is a foodie anyway? A foodie is a food fanatic. You qualify. Come hungry and stay awhile.

Hours

Daily . . . . 7 am - 10 pm

Cost

Varies

Location

I-10 west to Bonnabel Blvd. Turn right, go to Veterans Blvd. Turn right and go five blocks.

GABRIELLE

3201 Esplanade Ave.
504-948-6233

Contemporary Creole

You have to love a restaurant on the corner of Esplanade and Mystery St.

In a bright and inviting setting, Chef Greg Sonnier's imaginative cuisine runs the gamut from almond cracker crusted rabbit with crabmeat alfredo and smothered greens, to pan seared gulf fish with crawfish cornbread dressing and shrimp mousseline. You can play it safe and start with traditional turtle soup, or go crazy and try the seared foie gras on a pig's ear with pomegranate-blackberry molasses sauce. Really. Do not miss the buttermilk roasted garlic dressing for your salad.

Hours

Dinner:
Tuesday - Saturday . . . . 5:30-10:00 pm
Lunch (Oct. - May)
Tuesday - Saturday . . . . 11:30 am - 2 pm

Cost

Dinner entrees: $17-$29

Directions

From the French Quarter, take Esplanade to Mystery St.
(A few blocks from the main entrance to City Park.)

GALATOIRE'S
209 Bourbon Street
504-525-2021

Creole

If fine cooking takes practice, practice, practice, Galatoire's should have it perfected. They've been working on their French Creole specialties since 1905. Even though the fire has been lit almost 100 years, still call ahead a couple of hours if you want to order the singularly savory Creole bouillabaise. The shrimp remoulade is the best in the city and meat lovers must try the filet with bearnaise sauce. Still, the main event is seafood. After extensive renovations, the second floor is open for the first time since World War II. It may be old, but this place still rocks.

Hours

Tuesday - Saturday . . . . 11:30 am - 9 pm
Sunday . . . . Noon - 9 pm

Cost

Entrees: $13 - $24.75

Location

Just inside the French Quarter,
second block of Bourbon street.

GAUTREAU'S

1728 Soniat St.
504-899-7397

Nouvelle Creole

The building used to house a neighborhood pharmacy and some of the original fixtures and cabinetry are still in place, as are the pressed tin ceiling and oxblood walls. Now a unique dining spot, the pharmacist's cabinets are filled with restaurant accouterments. The menu changes several times a year, but if you have good timing you'll find chilled sweet corn broth with jumbo lump crabmeat and avocado. The jerked pork chops are excellent, but other less unusual items like filets or grilled tuna are pretty wonderful. It's small and fills up fast . . . dine early and don't leave until you've had lemon buttermilk cake with strawberry jam filling.

Hours

Monday - Saturday . . . . 6 - 10 pm

Cost

Entrees: $17 - $28

Directions

Take historic St. Charles Avenue uptown
past Napoleon Ave. Right turn on Soniat St.

GENGHIS KHAN

4053 Tulane Avenue
504-482-4044

Korean

The owner loves beautiful music and great food, so get ready for a most entertaining evening. Your waiter may be singing tunes from "Showboat" or an aria from "Pagliacci," while he's clearing your salad plates. A dramatic rendering of "The Phantom of the Opera" is accompanied by sounds of a lively, intimate dining room, usually filled to capacity. Best bet: the prix-fixe menu. Go for the crispy whole fish, softshell crab, whole lobster, or Steak Genghis Khan. Choose from six appetizers and enjoy the owner's enchanting violin.

Hours

Tuesday - Sunday . . . . 6-11 pm

Cost

Weeknights: $19.95
Weekends: $24.95

Directions

From downtown New Orleans take Tulane Avenue. Located near the corner of Tulane and Carrolton Ave.

THE GRILL ROOM

Windsor Court Hotel
504-522-1992

Fine Dining

Gentlemen, jackets please, and ladies, break out the little black dress because you finally have somewhere to show it off. This luxuriously appointed fine dining room features full breakfast, lunch, and dinner menus that change every day. The most fun is dinner, where the service is impeccable and the atmosphere lush and inviting. Great fish preparations are a staple here, and the wine list is among the best you will find in the South. Order the lobster and risotto and stay awhile. The chairs are so comfortable you might not want to give up your spot.

Hours

Breakfast . . . . 7 am - 10:30 am
Lunch . . . . 11:30 am - 2 pm
Dinner . . . . 6 pm - 10 pm

Cost

Lunch entrees . . . . $12 - $22.50
Dinner entrees . . . . $31 - $39

Directions

2nd floor the Windsor Court,
300 Gravier St.,
Central Business District

IRENE'S CUISINE
539 St. Philip Street
504-529-8811

Italian

From outside it looks like the old paper warehouse it was, but inside owner Irene DiPietro has created a warm Italian eatery that is always hopping. Irene's culinary life is a tribute to the wonders of garlic, rosemary, oregano, and such. You've likely never had chicken like hers, roasted with rosemary, garlic, and brandy, and if you want to know what manicotti is supposed to be all about, this is your place. Here it is generously plump with cheese and veal. If the place is so full you have to wait on the sidewalk outside, it's a festive corner. And it smells great.

Hours
Dinner
Sunday - Thursday . . . . 5:30 - 10:30 pm
Saturday & Sunday . . . . until 11

Cost
Entrees: $11.50 - $18.95

Directions
On the corner of Chartres and St. Philip Streets, one block from Decatur Street, French Quarter.

JOHNNY'S PO-BOYS

511 St. Louis Street
504-524-8129

New Orleans Po-Boy Sandwich

Johnny's is the kind of neighborhood place where you see some of the same faces every day. In fact, some of them have been coming ever since Mr. Johnny (DeGrusha) sliced his first loaf of French bread in 1950 and stuffed it generously with plump fried shrimp and oysters. Now lots of DeGrushas work there. Some come for daily lunch specials, hearty and spicy, including Monday's traditional red beans and rice, as well as things like spaghetti with huge meatballs or a seafood plate so full most mortals can't conquer it. *Good Housekeeping* once named Johnny's one of the top 100 of its kind in the country.

Hours

Daily . . . . .8 am - 4:30 pm

Cost

Prices vary . . . . $2.99 - $6

Directions

St. Louis street, right across Decatur from the Hard Rock Cafe, French Quarter.

K-PAUL'S LOUISIANA KITCHEN

416 Chartres St.
504-524-7394

Cajun

Renowned chef Paul Prudhomme's restaurant features strictly Louisiana cuisine. Balcony and courtyard seating are available, but the most fun is inside, watching the chefs at work in the display kitchen. They're preparing specialties like Bronzed Swordfish with Hot Fanny Sauce, Seafood Atchafalaya, Eggplant Pirogue Dauphine or Blackened Yellowfin Tuna, authentically cooked in a cast iron skillet. Walking distance to historic Jackson Square—you'll need the exercise after this dining experience.

Hours

Lunch: Monday - Saturday . . . . from 11:30 am
Dinner: Monday - Saturday . . . . from 5:30 pm

Cost

Lunch: Entrees, about $12
Dinner: Entrees, about $25

Directions

Between Conti and St. Louis streets, French Quarter.

MOSCA'S
4137 US 90
Waggaman, LA
504-436-9942

Creole / Italian

Mosca's is way, way off the beaten path, and far past the end of what is usually considered New Orleans territory, and easy to miss. It looks like a roadhouse with a lone beer sign hanging out front, but for decades locals have made the pilgrimage because the food is incomparable. The roasted chicken arrives with oversize chunks of garlic, sizzling on an iron platter. Order that, as well as the spaghetti bordelaise, the Italian shrimp, and the oysters Italian style, and pass everything around the table, family style. Insider's tip: Go hungry. Go VERY hungry, and be prepared to wait a long time for a table. It's worth it.

Hours

Reservations accepted only Tuesday through Saturday
Tuesday - Saturday . . . . 5:30 pm - 9:30 pm

Cost

About $30 per person

Directions

Take US 90 across the Crescent City bridge and continue west; keep a sharp lookout on the left-hand side of the road. It's hard to spot.

Best Bet: Ask a local to drive or call for detailed directions. It's well worth the journey.

MR. B'S
201 Royal Street
504-523 - 2078

Creole

A casually chic atmosphere accented by dark wood, glass, and green vinyl seating, Mr. B's is the home of New Orleans' power lunch, and much more. The energy of this place is a big draw, and the people-watching is the best in town. A typical lunch includes a coconut beer shrimp appetizer or fried oysters, followed by pasta jambalaya or paneed chicken and fettucine. Dinner starts best with Skillet Shrimp, marinated with roasted garlic and hickory grilled on a pepper biscuit. Best bets: garlic chicken or hickory grilled fish. Mr. B's invites you to "feed your spirit" at Sunday brunch, starting with mint julips and seafood gumbo. Hallelujah!

Hours

Lunch:
Monday - Friday . . . . 11:30 am - 3 pm
Dinner:
Nightly . . . . 5:30 - 10 pm
Rhythm 'n B's Brunch:
Sunday . . . . 11 am - 3 pm

Cost

Lunch: $11.50 - $15
Dinner: $16 - $23
Brunch: $12 - $14

Location

Just inside the French Quarter
on the corner of Royal and Bienville.

NAPOLEON HOUSE
500 Chartres Street
504-524-9752

New Orleans Traditional Quisine

From the outside looking in, Napoleon House looks dingy and crumbling, but the truth is it's one of the hottest spots in town. Best known for its Pimms Cup cocktail with the cucumber garnish, Napoleon House also offers sandwiches, soups, and a light menu. Stop in on a rainy day, order a warm muffalatta sandwich and drink in the history of a place that dates to the 19th-century and looks every day of its age. Oh, and about that name . . . Napoleon never saw this place— it was built two years after he died.

Hours

Monday - Thursday . . . . 11 am - Midnight
Frday - Saturday . . . . until 1 am
Sunday . . . . 11 am - 7pm

Cost

Varies

Directions

Corner of Chartres and St. Louis Streets, French Quarter.

OLD DOG NEW TRICK CAFE
307 Exchange Alley
504-522-4569

Vegetarian

If you still think meatless meals are not really meals at all, this place will change your mind and your palate. Billed as the restaurant "for vegetarians and curious carnivores," it was included in *Self Magazine's* list of the top six vegetarian restaurants in the U.S. The basics are there (tofu, black beans, etc.), but there are also polenta pizzas to die for, with toppings including Greek olives, rosemary, romano, mozzarella, onions, and tomatoes. Try Tuna to Tango, and definitely have the soups. The desserts naturally sweetened with maple syrup will surprise you.

Hours

Daily . . . . 11:30 am - 9 pm

Cost:
$7 - $10

Directions

Exchange Alley is in the French Quarter, between Chartres and Royal streets, bordered by Conti and Bienville Streets.

PALACE CAFE

605 Canal Street
504-523-1661

Creole/Cajun

Artfully blending Louisiana's two favorite cooking styles, the Palace is as popular with downtown business types as it is with visitors. Owned by the Brennans, New Orleans' first family of dining, this restaurant has an urban feel with just enough ambiance to remind you you're right on the edge of the French Quarter. Best bet for lunch: Gulf Shrimp Tchefuncte, sautéed with mushroom and scallions in Creole sauce. For dinner, be adventuresome with andouille sausage crusted gulf fish, accented by cayenne garlic sauce. Appetizer: Crabmeat cheesecake.

Dessert? Easy . . . white chocolate bread pudding smothered with warm chocolate ganache.

Hours

Lunch:
Monday - Friday . . . . 11:30 am - 2:30 pm

Dinner:

Nightly . . . . 5:30 - 10 pm

Jazz Brunch:

Saturday & Sunday . . . . 10:30 am - 2:30 pm

Cost

Lunch entrees: . . . . $12 - $15
Dinner entrees: . . . . $18 - $25

Location

Canal Street at the entrance to the French Quarter.

PASCAL'S MANALE

1828 Napoleon Avenue
504-895-4877

Italian/Seafood

Say the words Pascal's Manale to any New Orleanian and the first thing they think of is savory, spicey barbecued shrimp. Pascal's Manale has been serving them up forever, it seems, along with authentically prepared Italian dishes and outstanding seafood entrees. If you like pasta, this is your place. If you like pepper, these are your shrimp. And if you like the feel of an honest to goodness New Orleans neighborhood tradition with consistently fine food, this is your best bet.

Hours

Monday - Friday . . . . 11:30 am - 10 pm
Saturday . . . . 4 pm - 10 pm

Cost

Moderately priced—$25 buys a dinner fit for a king.

Directions

Take the streetcar up St. Charles Avenue to Napoleon Avenue. Walk north two blocks. Will be on the left.

PERISTYLE

1041 Dumaine St.
504-593-9535

Continental

Operating with the "less is more" approach, Peristyle has an intimate and elegant lounge, and a warm, simply furnished dining room. The food has the same simplicity about it, but it's creative and flavorful. The Sauté of Louisiana Oysters is served with crispy applewood bacon. The Veal Sweetbreads is a favorite among regulars, as is the grilled quail and the Tuna a la Anne, named for the quietly emerging chef, Anne Kearney. Insider's tip: Friday lunch turns into a party every week. Make a reservation well in advance.

Hours

Lunch
Friday only .. Two seatings: 11:30 am & 1 pm
Dinner
Tuesday - Saturday . . . . 6 - 10 pm

Cost

Friday lunch: $18
Dinner entrees: Avg. $23

Directions

Dumaine St. between Rampart and Burgundy, French Quarter.

PRALINE CONNECTION

90107 S. Peters Street   504-523-3973
542 Frenchman Street   504-943-3934

Southern Creole

You knew New Orleans had to have a great soul food restaurant, but you may not have known how much fun it is. It started as a place to carry out a quart of red beans or greens and grew into one of the city's most popular eateries. This is the place to bring the kids for barbecue ribs, fried chicken livers with brown gravy, meatloaf, stewed chicken or turkey wings. The S. Peters location has a spirited gospel Sunday brunch. Have some eggs and make a joyful noise.

Hours

S. Peters location:
Monday - Friday . . . . 11 am - 3 pm (lunch buffet)
Sunday Gospel brunch   11 am - 1 pm & 2 - 4 pm
Frenchman St. location:
Daily . . . . 11 am - 10:30 pm

Cost

St. Peters location:
Lunch - $9.80;   Brunch - $23.95
Frenchman St. location:
$5.95 - $24.95

Directions from downtown, Canal St.

Frenchman St. location:
Take Decatur St. through the French Quarter
until it becomes Frenchman.
Go two blocks and look for the red and white building.

S. Peters location:
From the French Quarter, take Charles Street one block
past Esplanade Avenue to Frenchman Street.

THE QUARTER SCENE RESTAURANT

900 Dumaine Street
504-522-6533

Neighborhood

From the outside it looks like the corner store in anytown, USA. Inside this quaint, cozy eatery is the toast of the neighborhood for French Quarter residents. Locals meet and mix with tourists at QSR, while dining on everything from veggie-burgers to pecan-crusted catfish, and fried shrimp po-boys to the most imaginative salads in town. Dinner specials are a constant surprise and might include Cajun stuffed chicken breast over wild rice, or good old southern fried chicken livers with mashed potatoes and gravy. Insider's tip: Sunday breakfast is a great way to start a French Quarter day—don't miss the big, crispy biscuits.

Hours

Closed Tuesdays

Daily . . . . .8 am - 12 midnight

Cost

$3.95 - $13.95

Directions

Corner of Dumaine and Dauphine Streets,
in the middle of the French Quarter.

UGLESICH'S

1238 Baronne Street
504-523-8571

Sandwiches/Seafood

In a city that loves comfort food, nothing is more comfortable than a big shrimp or oyster po-boy from Uglesich's. This place is 70 years old and it looks every day of that, and when you leave be prepared to smell like the restaurant. It's inevitable because inside these crumbling walls they fry seafood all day long. Oysters are shucked to order, the grilled fish plate is heavenly. Hearty eaters should have a hot roast beef po-boy and fries, or one of the phenomenal daily blackboard specials. Every trip to New Orleans needs at least one lunch at Uglesich's.

Hours

Monday - Friday . . . . 11 am - 4 pm

Cost

$6 - $14

Location

Baronne Street at Erato Street, one block off historic St. Charles Avenue, midtown.

WEST END CAFE

8536 Pontchartrain Blvd.
504-288-0711

Breakfast, Sandwiches, Seafood

Nothing fancy here, but get ready for great food. New Orleans is serious about its meatballs, and West End has one of the best meatball po-boys in town. Sports memorabilia and a rollicking atmosphere set the tone, and home-style cooking abounds. Try a daily special, such as Wednesday's chicken fried steak or Sunday's full roast turkey dinner with oyster and andouille sausage dressing. Best bets for seafood: Stuffed crabs, crawfish pie, or fried catfish. Kids eat cheap: A peanut butter and jelly sandwich . . . 95 cents. See? We knew you'd love this place.

Hours

Weekdays . . . . 10:30 am - 10:30 pm
Friday and Saturday . . . . until 11 pm

Cost

Breakfast: $.95 - $8.95
Lunch/Dinner: $2.95 - $15.95
Kids: Almost free!

Directions

I-10 west to West End Blvd. exit. Stay on West End Blvd. for 3 stoplights. At Robert E. Lee take a left and then the first right turn. You'll see West End Cafe.

IN THE FRENCH QUARTER:
175 **177** **178** **179** **180** **184** **187**

Chapter 7
WHERE TO STAY?

CLAIBORNE MANSION

2111 Dauphine Street
504-949-7327

This is the place you imagined yourself staying while visiting the Crescent City. A 19th-century mansion on the edge of Washington Square Park, and a minute walk from colorful, eclectic Frenchman Street in the Fauburg Marigny area. All the comforts and amenities are here, including a pool and a great courtyard, but the real attractions are the rooms. They're huge and each features a great four-poster bed. The neighborhood is one of those great old residential areas with terrific opportunities for after-dinner walks.

Speaking of dinner, try nearby Santa Fe, a sophisticated Southwestern eatery.

Cost

Rooms, $150; Suites, $210 - $300

Directions

From the French Quarter, take Dauphine Street into the Fauburg Marigny area.

COMFORT SUITES DOWNTOWN

346 Baronne Street
504-524-1140
800-524-1140

The real story of this hotel is one of saving money. Centrally located and well-kept, this is a no-frills hotel with all the services and amenities you'll need. Included are free newspapers, saunas, pay-laundry room, business services and safes in the rooms.Each room is called a suite with refrigerator and microwave. A quick walk to the streetcar and just a few blocks from the French Quarter.

Cost

Rates vary; as low as $150 at certain times of the year.

Directions

Baronne Street at Union and Perdido Streets.

DEGAS HOUSE BED AND BREAKFAST

2306 Esplanade Avenue
504-821-5009
800-755-6730

Edgar Degas' family owned this house, and he stayed in it in the latter 19th century. Today it has been lovingly and authentically restored as a charming bed and breakfast inn. Featuring 7 beautifully designed rooms on the second and third floors, each with a private bath. The house is decorated throughout with Degas artwork. Breakfast in the lush courtyard is one of the most peaceful moments you can spend in New Orleans.

Best bet: Try to reserve the chandeliered second floor guest room that features a balcony on the front of the house.

Cost
$125 - $200

Directions
From the French Quarter, take Esplanade Avenue to North Tonti St.

LAFAYETTE HOTEL

600 St. Charles Avenue
504-524-4441
800-733-4754

The beauty of this nearly century-old hotel is in the details. Beautiful brass accessories and polished marble everywhere add to the distinctive feel of a small hotel from another time. Upstairs from the small lobby, rooms are decorated with comfort and elegance in mind.

Best bet: Ask for a room with floor to ceiling windows that opens onto a private balcony.

Insider's tip: New Orleans Saints Coach Mike Ditka is soon to open his own restaurant on the first floor.

Cost

$175 and up, rates vary

Directions

Six blocks from Canal Street on St. Charles Avenue.

LE PAVILION HOTEL

833 Poydras Street
504-581-3111
800-535-9095

Le Pavilion is old, grand, and elegant, and almost museum-like in its stature, but it never takes itself too seriously. Consider the 10 pm ritual of peanut butter and jelly sandwiches, milk, and hot chocolate presented on silver trays, buffet style, in the lobby, every night. Or the Friday night swing dancing. It looks like a grand dame, but it rocks. Still, the rooms are generously appointed and comfy and the rooftop pool is great fun. From the imposing chandeliers in the lobby to the proliferation of fresh flowers throughout, Le Pavilion is in a class of its own.

Cost

$115 - $265; seasonal package rates available
Suites, $595 - $1495

Directions

Located in the center of Poydras Street,
Central Business district, Downtown.

LE RICHELIEU

1234 Chartres Street
504-529-2492
800-535-9653

If you want a small hotel (69 rooms, 17 suites) with big hotel amenities and service, check in here. The rooms vary in decor and amenities, with some even featuring refrigerators and big walk-in closets. The place has a real feeling of privacy and the staff respects yours. Just a short walk away is the French Market, and the touristy part of the French Quarter is just far enough away. If you want to know what it's like to be a French Quarter resident, this is your place. A great bonus: free parking.

Best bet: Early morning, walk a few blocks down to Jackson Square for coffee and croissants at La Madeleine French Bakery and Cafe. Then step outside and have your palm read. Hey, it's New Orleans,

Cost
$120 - $170 (rooms)
$190 - $575 (suites)

Directions
Chartres Street at Barracks, French Quarter.

McKENDRICK-BREAUX HOUSE

1474 Magazine Street
504-586-1700

The owners could give lessons on operating a bed and breakfast. So authentically restored and professionally operated is this place, it seems they were born to do this. Gorgeous antiques and fresh flowers are everywhere, which makes sense since this 19th-century Greek Revival house is situated in the heart of the Magazine Street antiques district. A tip of the technological hat to the 20th century has been made in the form of voice mail and fax machines, but turn it all off and enjoy the luxurious garden and the oversize rooms with private entrances.

Best bet for a fun day: A shopping trip where you never leave Magazine Street—coffee at PJ's, 3000 Magazine (in an old orphanage); pasta for lunch at Semolina's, 3242 Magazine; and browsing for antiques all up and down the street. Hint: Comfortable shoes required.

Cost
$110 - $175

Directions
From downtown, take Magazine Street to Race Street.

MELROSE MANSION

937 Esplanade Avenue
504-944-2255

The Melrose Mansion is a regal presence on a corner bordering the French Quarter and the Fauburg Marigny area. The architecture is definitely part of the neighborhood, but the building is distinctive because of its bright white exterior and well-cared-for grounds. The four rooms and four suites all have high ceilings, shiny wood floors, elegant linens, and lavishly appointed bathrooms. The downstairs drawing room is a step into a more gracious era. Melrose Mansion is the way life is supposed to be.

Cost

$225 and up, rates vary.

Directions

Corner of Esplanade Avenue
and Burgundy Street, French Quarter.

HOTEL MAISON DE VILLE AND THE AUDUBON COTTAGES

727 Toulouse Street
504-561-5858
800-634-1600

This hotel is what Dan Akroyd, Tennessee Williams, and Elizabeth Taylor have in common, in case you were wondering. They and other notables have stayed in this private, peaceful oasis in the French Quarter. The hotel occupies a townhouse and slave quarters and features an elegant courtyard and a stellar restaurant, The Bistro. The seven cottages are a couple of blocks from the hotel, off the beaten path, and each has its own patio. The ambiance and furnishing are an easy step into the grandeur of the 19th century, but the real draw here is the impeccable service.

Cost
$215 - $375

Directions
Royal Street to Toulouse, French Quarter.

HOTEL MONTELEONE

214 Royal Street
504-523-3341
800-535-9595

The oldest hotel in the French Quarter is arguably also the finest. The grandeur of old New Orleans is alive and well at the foot of Royal Street in this piece of living history. Built in 1866 and meticulously maintained since, the hotel has been operated by the same family from the beginning. The rooms are uncommonly generous in square footage and no detail of ambiance or service is missed. Every item a guest comes in contact with is of the highest quality. No need to travel far for a great dinner. The Hunt Room Grill is just downstairs, as is the historic revolving Carousel Bar. Come on . . . go for a spin.

Cost

Seasonal rates start at $90; suites to $400

Directions

Just inside the French Quarter,
second block of Royal Street.

HOLIDAY INN - CHATEAU LE MOYNE

301 Dauphine Street
504-581-1303
800-465-4329

Although this French Quarter hotel has 160 rooms, the real attraction here is the eight suites located in Creole Cottages. The hotel is a French Quarter gem, located a few blocks into the Quarter, but far enough from the crowds. The rooms are lovely, but not overdone. The winding staircases and old-world decor set the tone for an ideal French Quarter vacation. Close to everything that matters.

Best bet Guests on a budget are welcome, and those looking for luxury will find it here, too

Take a one-block walk to Bayona, Chef Susan Spicer's elegant eatery, for lunch or dinner.

Cost

$250 and up.

Directions

Three blocks into the French Quarter on Dauphine St.

HOTEL INTER-CONTINENTAL

444 St. Charles Avenue
504-525-5566
800-445-6563

Sleek, sophisticated, contemporary and centrally located, Hotel Inter-Continental is right on the streetcar line. The hotel is an easy walk to the French Quarter or the Riverfront and the Warehouse District. All the amenities are here . . . health club, pool, mini-bars, and the liveliest Sunday jazz brunch in the city. Best bet: Make a reservation way in advance for Mardi Gras. This hotel just happens to be on the main parade route for Carnival. Get a seat in the private reviewing stands outside the main entrance. Later, have a Mardi Gras feast at the all-day buffet in the ballroom.

Cost

Rack rates: $250 and up.
Seasonal package rates starting at $125.

Directions

From Canal Street take St. Charles Avenue
just a few blocks.

PONTCHARTRAIN HOTEL

2031 St. Charles Avenue
504-524-0481
800-777-6163

The true New Orleans experience includes a suite at the Pontchartrain, a streetcar ride to view the dozens of historic mansions on the avenue, and dinner in the Caribbean Room in the hotel. After dinner, spend a lazy evening by the piano bar. The suites are all named for celebrities or dignitaries who have stayed there. This is a quiet, understated place that blends in with the neighborhood. No big happy hours or raucous events here—just subtle, European elegance that has had more than half a century to perfect itself. Practice has indeed made perfect.

Cost
$150 - $275

Directions
St. Charles Avenue, midtown, at Josephine Street.

QUALITY INN MAISON ST. CHARLES

1319 St. Charles Avenue
504-522-0187
800-831-1783

You'd never know you were steps away from historic St. Charles Avenue, the street that never sleeps. The buildings that make up this hotel have intimacy, privacy, and great courtyards to enjoy morning coffee or a full Louisiana moon. Walk from the hotel to the streetcar stop in minutes and take a scenic ride all the way uptown and back. In the evening, choose from the many recently opened restaurants in the area, or make your way to the Quarter with a ten-minute cab ride. With 113 rooms and 16 suites, the hotel is just big enough to satisfy all your needs and still small enough to feel cozy.

Entertainment tip: Go six blocks toward downtown and spend a lively evening at Le Chat Noir, New Orleans' newest cabaret. Right this way, your table's waiting.

Cost
$100 - $200

Directions
From downtown, take St. Charles Avenue to midtown.

SONIAT HOUSE

1133 Chartres Street
504-522-0570
800-544-8808

Once you enter these two 19th-century Creole townhouses through the carriageway, you're in another world. Your mind tells you you're in the French Quarter, but your eyes tell you you've time traveled to a more gracious era of refined service, charming settings, and European and Louisiana antiques. From the Egyptian cotton sheets to the books provided in each room, no detail is overlooked. Guests in each of the 25 rooms are attended to as if they were visiting dignitaries.

Best bet: Have your breakfast each morning in the luxuriant courtyard beneath the banana trees. Because you're worth it.

Cost

$160 - $250; Suites, $275 - $625

Directions

Near Chartres and Ursuline Streets, French Quarter.

THE CHIMES BED AND BREAKFAST

1146 Constantinople
504-488-4640
800-729-4640

The best part of staying in this fabulous uptown house may be the big family-style breakfast served every morning. Even staying for a weekend, guests tend to feel like a part of this place. The main house and carriage house are each meticulously maintained. High ceilings and hardwood floors combine to create the warm atmosphere here. All the rooms have private entrances. All the conveniences are here without the crowds. Enjoy the distinctive architecture in the neighborhood as you walk the nearby streets. Not far from the great antique rows on Magazine Street or the magic of St. Charles Avenue in the Garden District.

Cost
Less than $100 - $150

Directions
Constantinople and Coliseum Street, Garden District.

THE COLUMNS HOTEL

3811 St. Charles Avenue
504-899-9308

The Columns gets our vote for best place to stay uptown for Mardi Gras. If you think you've seen the building you probably have, because it's been in some well-known movies, such as *Pretty Baby* with Brooke Shields. The massive front porch features white tablecloth service, and the grand staircase inside is breathtaking. You won't mind the absence of a television in your room because who comes to New Orleans to watch TV? The Columns is a huge Victorian mansion and the porch is about the best place to watch Mardi Gras parades go by. The neighborhood is rich in architecture and ripe for long walks. Several fun restaurants are within walking distance, but you may elect to hop on the streetcar just outside the front door.

Cost

$90 - $200

Directions

St. Charles Avenue to General Taylor Avenue, Uptown.

THE ROYAL SONESTA HOTEL

300 Bourbon Street
504-586-0300
800-766-3782

If there's a better place to be right in the middle of Mardi Gras madness and still have the luxurious old-world elegance of a classic New Orleans hotel, we don't know where it would be. The Royal Sonesta, with its balconies overlooking Bourbon Street, is as elegant as it is raucous. The 500-room, 32-suite hotel takes up almost an entire block. It is home to two great restaurants, including Begue's, a room that successfully mixes classic French and traditional New Orleans foods. Great fitness facilities, business center, and a nightclub called The Can-Can Cafe and Jazz Club.

Cost

Singles/Doubles, $145 - $320; Suites to $1200

Directions

Three blocks into the French Quarter,
corner of Bourbon and Bienville Streets.

Chapter 8
WATCH FOR THESE ANNUAL EVENTS

January

February

March

April

May

June

July

August

September

October

November

December

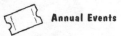

January
SUGAR BOWL

Louisiana's oldest annual sporting event originated in 1935. Not only is the event the most famous of college football games, it has grown to include championships for tennis, soccer, basketball, sailing, running, and flag football. It's now one of the largest athletic events in the country, held generally on New Year's Day in the Superdome. Ask for the ticket office (504-525-8573).

January
BATTLE OF NEW ORLEANS CELEBRATION

Each year, the city celebrates its victory at the Battle of New Orleans in 1815. Volunteers commemorate a living history. British and American encampments, artillery firing demonstrations (muskets and cannons), and tours of the Chalmette Battlefield attract thousands. The battlefield is now part of the Jean Lafitte National Historical Park and Preserve. The event takes place on the weekend nearest the battle's anniversary—January 8. (The war was officially over when the Battle of New Orleans was fought.)

Shuttle buses meet visitors at the St. Bernard Parish Government Complex at 8201 W. Judge Peréz Drive in Chalmette. Admission is free (504-589-4428).

January
CARNIVAL SEASON

Weeks of parades and private masquerades precede Mardi Gras Day, known as Carnival season. It officially begins on January 6—the Twelfth Night or the Feast of the Epiphany— and ends the day before Ash Wednesday. Carnival colors—purple, green, and gold—glorify the city. Watch the daily newspaper *Times Picayune* for parade routes and times.

January
LUNDI GRAS

A newer carnival tradition, Lundi Gras or "Fat Monday," heralds the beginning of Mardi Gras from the Spanish Plaza across from the Riverwalk Marketplace. The event swings into action with a parade, fireworks, free outdoor concerts and the court arriving by riverboat (504-522-1555).

February
NEW ORLEANS BOAT & SPORTSFISHING SHOW

The latest models of boats at the Superdome make their debut at the largest regional boat show, along with boating paraphernalia: engines, fishing gear, electronics, recreational equipment. Held the last weekend in February (504-846-4446).

February
MARDI GRAS

Over a million people hit the streets on New Orleans' biggest day. Crowds pack the French Quarter and Canal Street; but families wanting to escape the ruckus head for St. Charles Ave. and Veterans Blvd. Parades and activities crank up early and continue after dark. Mardi Gras, "Fat Tuesday," takes place each year, always 46 days before Easter. (Ash Wednesday starts 45 days of Lent.) Hotels book up as much as a year in advance for Mardi Gras weekend, Friday through Tuesday (800-672-6124 or 504-566-5003).

March
ST. PATRICK'S DAY PARADE

With St. Patrick's Day on the 17th (504-525-5169) and the Feast Day of St. Joseph on the 19th, activities coincide for a week of parades, food, and festivities. Traditions on these holidays aren't your normal tourist stuff, but those of the strong ethnic communities in New Orleans. It's an Irish

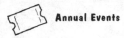
tradition to throw Irish foods at paraders: cabbages, onions, carrots, and potatoes. The parade begins on Decatur at the Market and runs through the French Quarter

The Sicilian descendants build altars covered with food in honor of their patron saint in homes, churches, restaurants, and businesses. You'll find one of these altars at the American Italian Museum at 537 S. Peters St. or check the newspaper for places to visit altars (504-522-7294).

March
TENNESSEE WILLIAMS FESTIVAL

For three days around the third week in March, writers and scholars flock to New Orleans for a series of theatrical productions, readings, lectures, and a literary walking tour focused on Tennessee Williams. Events take place at different locations, mostly in the French Quarter. Highlight: the Stella Hollering Contest at Jackson Square (504-581-1144).

April
FRENCH QUARTER FESTIVAL

The French Quarter awakens each spring with festivities for food and music lovers. Enjoy the "world's largest jazz brunch" (a huge array of food booths and jazz performers in Jackson Square & Woldenberg Park), fireworks over the Mississippi River, courtyard tours, an array of popular local musicians on stages, and the waiters' race. Waiters, carrying trays, race through the streets of the French Quarter. Festivities include children's activities. Held the 2nd weekend in April, preceding the New Orleans Jazz and Heritage Festival (504-522-5730).

April
NEW ORLEANS JAZZ AND HERITAGE FESTIVAL

One of the world's great celebrations, held for 10 days during the last weekend of April and the 1st weekend of

May, at the New Orleans' Fair Ground and other music venues around town. The New Orleans Jazz & Heritage Festival (Jazz Fest) consists of the Louisiana Heritage Fair and the Evening Concert Series. Many a big-name star performs with other big names in the audience. Top chefs show off their regional cooking; first-class artists and craftsmen, their wares. Purchase tickets for concerts and make hotel reservations months in advance (504-522-4786). Call Ticketmaster (504-522-5555).

May
LOUISIANA CRAWFISH FESTIVAL

The "mudbug" takes center stage at this popular annual festival in the heart of Cajun country in Breaux Bridge. Claiming to be the "Crawfish Capital of the World," the community swings into action with food, music, art, craft booths, and lots of atmosphere. Held the 1st full week in May, over 100,000 attend this event. Breaux Bridge is located west of New Orleans, exit Highway 31 South from I-10 (20 miles east of Lafayette) (337-332-5406.)

May
GREEK FESTIVAL

Annually held at the Hellenic Cultural Center at the Greek Orthodox Cathedral of the Holy Trinity, 1200 Robert E. Lee Blvd. at St. Bernard Avenue, on the weekend before Memorial Day weekend in May, this popular, well-attended festival spoils visitors with tasty foods, folk dancing, and crafts—that's all Greek (504-282-0259.)

June
GREAT FRENCH MARKET
TOMATO FESTIVAL

On the first weekend of June, the French Market celebrates the Louisiana Creole tomato with food specialties prepared by local restaurants. Food booths

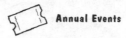
line the French Market on Decatur and feature cooking demonstrations and sampling. Local musicians entertain throughout the day (504-522-2621).

June
REGGAE RIDDUMS INTERNATIONAL ARTS FESTIVAL

What was once only a regional event now draws national attention. A three-day music lover's feast, the Reggae Riddums, held in City Park, showcases the best in reggae, calypso, and soca musicians. Enjoy authentic island foods and traditional Caribbean crafts (504-367-1313).

July
GO 4TH ON THE RIVER

New Orleans' Independence Day celebration takes in the Riverfront (Woldenberg Park) from the French Market to the Riverwalk Marketplace. Plenty of local music and cuisine: alligator-on-a-stick, shrimp jambalaya, gumbo. Attractions along the riverfront (John James Audubon Riverboat, Aquarium of Americas, Entergy IMAX Theatre, and Mardi Gras World) discount admissions. Shops and restaurants add to the merriment with specials. Fireworks from barges on the river (504-528-9994).

August
WHITE LINEN NIGHT

For one evening, the first Saturday in August, art galleries in the Warehouse/Art District hold a block party. Vendors along Julia Street offer fine foods while attendees enjoy performances by the New Orleans Opera or the Louisiana Philharmonic Orchestra. Good time to buy art at bargain prices (504-523-1216).

October
ART FOR ART'S SAKE

The New Orleans art community kicks off its cultural season with citywide gallery openings on the 1st Saturday in October. Evening events at the Contemporary Arts Center feature a party with live music, dancing, and food, as their annual fundraiser (504-523-1216).

October
SWAMP FESTIVAL

Here's your chance to get friendly with the swamp critters at the Audubon Zoo. The festivities, held the 1st and 2nd weekends in October, feature Cajun food, live music, and heritage crafts at the Audubon Zoo and at Woldenberg Riverfront Park (504-861-2537).

October
GUMBO FESTIVAL

A three-day festival is held at Angel Square in Bridge City, across the river from New Orleans. Featuring Cajun food, continuous live entertainment, free admission and parking (504-436-4712).

October
GHOSTLY GALLIVANT

A popular annual fundraiser sponsored by the Friends of the Cabildo a week before Halloween. Self-guided tours of favorite ghost haunts in the French Quarter. Not too spooky, great for families. Historical as well as lots of fun (504-523-3939).

November
DESTREHAN PLANTATION FALL FESTIVAL

The 2nd weekend in November a festival featuring food, crafts, antique dealers, and a tour of the old manor make for a pleasant drive into the countryside. This old plantation on River Road is located 20 miles west of New Orleans in Destrehan (504-764-9315).

November
CELEBRATION IN THE OAKS

New Orleans captures the Christmas spirit every year at City Park. Lights glow from the many ancient oaks, and the two-mile drive through the park makes for a New Orleans-style Christmas tradition. Be sure to ride the miniature train through the park; it claims to be the longest miniature train ride in the country, and this is the only time it runs after dark. Walk through the botanical garden, enjoy nightly visits from Santa, and take a horse-drawn carriage through the park (504-483-9411).

November
ALL SAINTS DAY

November 1st marks the day when the great "Cities of the Dead"—the cemeteries in New Orleans—come alive when many city residents come out to clean and decorate the old tombstones. This is the best time to visit these old secluded cemeteries that are otherwise unsafe.

December
A NEW ORLEANS CHRISTMAS

Citywide events celebrate the holiday season. Each year the festivities increase with significance from a means of drawing in tourists during the slow month of December. The entire month is filled with concerts, parades, children's programs, walking tours, cooking demonstrations, and riverboat cruises. Low hotel rates and special discounts at restaurants (504-522-5730).

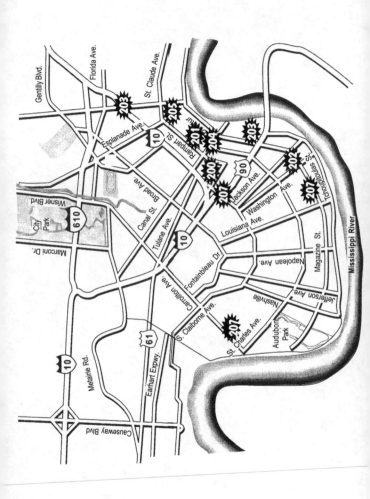

Chapter 9
SHOPPING IN NEW ORLEANS

ANTIQUE SHOPS

Let's Go Antiquing

Macon Riddle
504-899-3027

If you enjoy antique shopping and would like to spend the afternoon with a professional antique shopper, call Macon Riddle. She will help you find great buys. *neworleansantiquing.com*

New Orleans Auction

510 Julia St. (at Magazine St.)
504-566-1849

Auctions take place every 7 to 8 weeks, but the estate antiques are available for public viewing two weeks prior. Browse through the items; if you like something, simply leave them a bid. (They arrange shipping anywhere.) Here's a great place for finding antique jewelry, glass, rare books, sculpture, paintings, silver, and fine antiques.

The Royal Street Guild

504-524-1260
www.royalstreetguild.com

The Royal Street Guild, a merchant association, provides informative brochures on antique shops on Royal Street. Antique shopping on Royal Street is considered some of the best shopping in the world. Look for their brochure in hotels and shops or call to schedule a tour.

ART GALLERIES

Martin LaBorde Gallery

509 Royal Street (between St. Louis and Toulouse Sts.)
504-587-7111

Many New Orleanians speculate that the up-and-coming artist Martin LaBorde will be the next Louisiana superstar. His paintings of the wizard Bodo thrill art lovers everywhere and his works have been exhibited in many major cities: Tokyo, Munich, Mexico City, and Chicago. See several of his pieces at the Upperline Restaurant in the Uptown District.

Rodrigue Gallery of New Orleans

721 Royal Street (at Orleans St.)
504-581-4244
www.bluedogart.com

Folks stop dead in their tracks on Royal Street when faced with one of George Rodrique's paintings of the "Blue Dog." Open since 1989, his galleries exclusively sell his works. The artist, a native of southern Louisiana, frequently makes visits. His paintings continue to grow in popularity and have become symbolic of contemporary American culture with its roots deep in Cajun history. The gallery is located in the French Quarter behind the St. Louis Cathedral. Books by the artist are also for sale. New to Louisiana is the Blue Dog Café, opening in Lafayette, Louisiana, and featuring much of his personal collection. The artist, however, sells his works only out of his galleries.

BOOK STORES

Beaucoup Books

5414 Magazine Street (at Jefferson St.)
504-895-2663 or 800-543-4114.

A favorite stop for booklovers, offering a large selection of local and regional titles. French and Spanish editions are another specialty. A separate room houses the children's selection. The store features upcoming literary events and signings.

Faulkner House Books

624 Pirate's Alley (between Chartres and Royal Sts.)
504-524-2940

Shop for books at the former residence of William Faulkner. He wrote his first novel, *Soldiers' Pay*, here. The shop sells many of his works, including some first editions. It also headquarters a literary society and specializes in New Orleans and Louisiana histories.

Garden District Book Shop

2727 Prytania St. (at Washington Ave.)
504-895-2266

This shop carries Anne Rice's books; many signed by the author, and many limited editions. It also specializes in rare books on Louisiana and New Orleans.

Librairie Bookshop

823 Chartres Street (between Dumaine and St. Ann Sts.)
504-525-4837

Second hand/out-of-print books are this shop's specialty; in fact, it's one of the best haunts for rare books in the city. Things to browse for are old postcards and local titles. A favorite with many New Orleanians for over 25 years.

FOOD MARKETS

Central Grocery Company

923 Decatur Street (between Philips and Dumaine Sts.)
504-523-1620

Established by Italian immigrants, Central Grocery created the original muffalatta and made culinary history. Now a very popular lunching spot, this mom-and-pop store is packed with all kinds of imported products. A great place if you're loading up goodies for a picnic or the trip back home.

Spice, Inc.

1051 Annunciation Street (Warehouse District)
504-558-9992

Offers a wide variety of specialty foods and a cooking school. Classes at the cooking school are taught evenings and during the day. Susan Spicer and guest chefs teach the classes, $30-$45. Kids' cooking classes make for fun Saturdays twice a month, $20. The store features imported cheeses, exotic spices, freshly baked breads, pastries, and produce. But it's the take-outs and the deli café, open daily 11am - 3 pm, that will make it one of your routine stops.

Whole Foods Market

3135 Esplanade Avenue (at Mystery St.)
504-943-1626

A national chain store, Whole Foods Market sells a large variety of baked goodies, nuts, grains, granolas, cheeses, and other health food products. What's most popular is their deli counter. The store offers many kinds of specialty sandwiches and prepared dishes.

MASK SHOPS

Little Shop of Fantasies
523 Dumaine Street (between Chartres and Decatur Sts.)
504-529-4243

It's Mardi Gras any day of the year at this clever little shop filled with handmade leather masks. This is a shop that deserves a visit.

Masquerade Fantasy
1233 Decatur Street
(between Governor Nicholls and Barracks Sts.)
504-593-9269

Serious stuff. Artist Jim Gibeault sells some of the best designed masks in New Orleans. His masks made of leather are handcrafted and hand-painted. It's fun to browse through his fanciful creations.

MUSIC SHOPS

Louisiana Music Factory
210 Decatur Street (between Iberville and Bienville Sts.)
504-586-1094

Considered to have the largest selection of jazz music anywhere, the Louisiana Music Factory also has a knowledgeable staff. They'll tell you what you need to know when it comes to local and regional music. The second floor contains a huge selection of old records.

Record Ron's
239 Chartres Street
(between Iberville and Bienville Sts.)
504-522-2239

You'll find a large selection of local and regional music as well as new releases. Famous for their collections of oldies.

UNIQUE SHOPS

American Aquatic Gardens
621 Elysian Fields Avenue
(between Royal and Chartres Sts.)
504-944-0410

Visitors find the American Aquatic Gardens an important last stop before heading home. This commercial outfit's focus is water gardening, and they sell stone ornaments, pond kits, handmade fountains, and tropical plants. Water lilies are the most popular with tourists and can be wrapped for travel. The gift shop's a highlight, with lots of one-of-a-kind items. If gardening is your stuff, be sure to stop in.

Aunt Sally's Praline Shop
810 Decatur Street (between St. Ann and Dumaine Sts.)
504-524-3373

You may find this slick little shop a bit touristy, but it's actually a great place to buy regional cookbooks, fresh pralines, and other mementos for the trip back home. It is located next door to Café du Monde. The cookbook *Creole Gumbo and All That Jazz* by Howard Mitcham is a favorite.

Bergen Galleries
730 Royal Street (at Orleans St.)
504-523-7882

If you want it, they have it. Their extensive collection of images will simply blow your mind. With over 12,000 on hand, the gallery makes for an art lover's supermarket. Sections in the store cover a wide range of subjects: New Orleans, Louisiana, Mardi Gras, jazz, food, sports and more. The gallery specialties include New Orleans Jazz and Heritage Festival and Mardi Gras collectibles.

Fleur de Paris
712 Royal St. (at Pirate's Alley)
504-525-1899

One of the most innovative shops in New Orleans for women's apparel. You'll find elegant designer dresses and custom-made hats. Pick a basic hat— straw or felt—and trim it from hundreds of ribbons, flowers, veils, lace, and plumage.

Louisiana Children's Museum Gift Shop
420 Julia St. (at Constance St.)
504-523-1357

You'll find interesting items: a scientific hot air balloon that stands 5 feet tall; a rocket that shoots over a 100 feet high; kits for creating your own perfume, building a crystal radio, and for fingerprinting; and tons of popular books.

Old Town Pralines
627 Royal Street (between St. Peter and Toulouse Sts.)
504-525-1413

The pralines are tasty, but you can't beat this little shop's vintage atmosphere. You'll find old pictures of the old French Opera House that once stood around the corner from this shop. It burnt down in 1919. Other memorabilia recalls one of the French Quarter's greatest love stories. In 1860, Adelina Patti took New Orleans by storm. Her performances sold out as she broke the hearts of many a Creole gentleman. She was very well known in Europe.

Whisnant's
222 Chartres Street (between Iberville and Bienville Sts.)
504-524-9766

You'll find yourself fascinated with all the unusual collectibles that fill this store. Very eclectic, the inventory includes 9th century and earlier arms and armor, a miniature Dutch carousel, ethnic jewelry from Africa, a 7-foot folk art steam ship, and mirror furniture.

UNIQUE PLACES TO SHOP

Canal Place Shopping Center

333 Canal Street (at Tchoupitoulas St.)
504-522-9200

The Westin Canal Place Hotel, with its fantastic view of the river, tops this fanciful high-rise shopping mall, where you'll find the best collection of department and clothing stores in town. It is also home to the Southern Repertory Theatre and Canal Place Cinema. You'll find Rhino, a gallery filled with original craftwork by 80 different local artists. Take advantage of their reasonable all-day parking rates; the lot puts you within easy walking distance of the French Quarter, the Warehouse/Art District, the Central Business District and the Riverfront. Mall shops and attractions (like the Aquariums of America). All will validate your ticket.

French Quarter and French Market

Bounded by the Mississippi River, Canal Street,
Rampart Street, and Espanade Avenue

The French Quarter and its French Market is always a shoppers paradise. The endless assortment of shops and restaurants represent the local culture and cuisine, as well as offering first class antiques, art, designer dresses, and collectibles. Royal Street is renowned for its galleries, antiques, and food. Don't overlook the funky off-beat shops on Chartres Street between Iberville and Jackson Square.

Jackson (Jax) Brewery and Millhouse
620-624 Decatur Street (at St. Peter St.)
504-7245 or 504-586-8015

What was once Jax Brewery from 1891-1974 now houses over 50 shops and eateries plus a food court: Planet Hollywood, Bayou Country General Store, Cookin' on the River, and the Hard Rock Café (located in a separate building), to name a few. Popular with visitors are the New Orleans School of Cooking and Louisiana General Store. A three-hour class is taught by local chefs. Experts teach gumbo, Jambalaya, and praline-making, with a fanciful feast at the end. Simply sign up for a one of their classes and come hungry.

Magazine Street

Magazine Street offers about 6 miles (from Canal St. to the Audubon Zoo) of shops and eateries. The 5900 block makes fun shopping for antiques, books, vintage jewelry, hats, and art. The 3900 block offers funky and elegant antiques, galleries, artists' studios, garden accessories, weaving, oriental rugs, and po-boy sandwiches. Look for the Useless Antique Shop and Old Books in the 3100 block. It's not advisable to walk Magazine Street, do it by car. Walking between these cluster of shops may be unsafe.

Maple Street

Commonly known as the Riverbend area, you'll find an array of dandy little shops that beg for attention. Maple Street's six blocks of shops (from Carrollton Avenue to Cherokee Street) are housed in turn-of-the-century restored cottages.

New Orleans Centre

1400 Poydras St. (between Loyola Ave. and LaSalle St.)
504-568-0000

New Orleans' swankiest place for shopping is located inside a pink skyscraper. It connects to the Superdome and the Hyatt Regency Hotel and consists of over 60 stores and restaurants. Sleep, shop, and enjoy entertainment without ever leaving air-conditioned comfort.

Riverwalk Marketplace

1 Poydras St.
(on the river, between Poydras and Girod Sts.)
504-522-1555

This wonderful shopping mall on the riverfront made national headlines when a freighter sideswiped it in 1996. No one was killed, but millions of dollars of damage occurred. The Bright Field, loaded with corn on its way to Japan, lost power and demolished parts of the mall and the adjoining New Orleans Hilton Riverside Hotel. The mall runs 1/2 mile along the riverfront from Canal Street to the Convention Center.

Great River Road Plantations

When it comes to elegant old plantations on River Road, if you have seen one, you haven't seen them all. Two of these plantations, Oak Alley and Nottoway, have excellent restaurants. Only Nottoway and Madewood plantations offer overnight stays right inside the mansions. If you love history, you'll find the guided tour at Laura Plantation fascinating. The San Francisco Plantation allows visitors to bring a picnic lunch to munch on while soaking up the lovely surroundings.

Chapter 10
PLANTATION, CAJUN & BAYOU COUNTRY

DESTREHAN PLANTATION

13034 River Road
Destrehan, Louisiana
504-764-9315

Once the home of French aristocrats

It took three years to build the raised cottage on the Destrehan Plantation. Considering that it was 1787, three years wasn't long at all. Well constructed, the house was made of cypress wood and brick with a West Indies style roof, all cut and fashioned by hand.

The house was first built in the French Colonial Style, but later in 1840 it was remodeled in the popular style of the day, Greek Revival. Nowadays it's been carefully restored and furnished with beautiful period antiques. The grounds of magnificent oaks draped with moss simply enhance the beauty of the old plantation house. Once an indigo plantation, in later years its primary crop was sugar cane.

If history and old plantation homes are of interest, the Destrahan Plantation, the oldest documented plantation in the Lower Mississippi Valley, is a must. The house may seem familiar; it was used in the filming of *Interview with a Vampire*. It is now listed on the National Registry of Historic Places.

Hours
Closed major holidays
Daily .... 9 am - 4 pm

Cost
Adults $7
Children .... 6-12 yrs . .$2; 13-17 yrs. .$4

Direction
8 mi. from the New Orleans International Airport on Hwy 48 (River Rd) or ½ mi. east of the Destrehan Bridge.

SAN FRANCISCO PLANTATION

Highway 44
Garyville, Louisiana 70051
225-535-2341 or 888-322-1756

Brightly colored plantation house in "steam-boat gothic" style

The San Francisco plantation house isn't typical antebellum. Its ornate style and bright colors remind many of a Mississippi riverboat. Inspired by its looks, the novelist Francis Parkinson Keyes wrote *Steamboat Gothic*, a story about a family she imagined living there.

The San Francisco Plantation Foundation, a Louisiana non-profit organization, now owns the San Francisco plantation house. After years of neglect, the house has been fully restored and is listed on the National Register of Historic Places. Tours are offered daily. Tables available for picnicking.

Hours

Daily .... 10 am (Last tour at 4:30 pm)

Cost

Adults	$7.50
Children 13-17	$4
Children 6-12	$3
Children under 5	Free

Directions

Located 45 minutes from New Orleans. Take 1-10 west, exit 206 at LaPlace. Take Highway 3188 south to Highway 61 and go right for 5 lights. At the 5th light, go left on Central Avenue. Follow until it dead ends onto Highway 44 (River Road). Go 3.4 miles. Will be on the right.

ST. JAMES HISTORICAL SOCIETY, CULTURAL & HERITAGE MUSEUM

1988 Highway 44
Lutcher, Louisiana 70071
225-869-9752

Interesting museum, local artifacts

Established in 1984, the St. James Museum highlights the history of River Road.

Rich in artifacts pertinent to the area, the museum's collection includes everything from sugar mill, Indian, plantation, and railroad memorabilia to old photographs. Housed in 150-year-old cottage, the museum also makes itself an authority on the St. James Bonfire Tradition. In many river communities, this has been a tradition for more than 200 years. Bonfires along the river levee on the weekend before winter solstice are believed to bring back the sun.

Hours

Weekdays . . . . 8 am - 4 pm
Weekends . . . . By appointment only

Cost

Free

Directions

From New Orleans, take I-10 west to exit #194 (Gramercy). Turn right on Hwy 3125. Turn right on Hwy 20. Continue to Hwy 44, turn right. Will be ½ mile on the right.

LAURA: A CREOLE PLANTATION

2247 Highway 18 River Road
Vacherie, Louisiana 70090
225-265-7690

Creole family's plantation

You'll have a good idea of what life was like on a sugar cane plantation in the early 1800's, once you take this tour. All the facts have been carefully researched from documents stored at the Archives Nationals de Paris and from former owner Laura Locoul's journal *"Memories of My Ole Plantation House."* The tour lasts 45 minutes.

The family lived on the plantation during the growing season from Easter to Christmas, then moved to the French Quarter during the winter months. The Creoles were influenced by many different cultures: West African, Spanish, French, and American Indian. The original old slave quarters still exist. The stories of "Br'er Rabbit" originated here.

Hours

(Closed Major holidays including Mardi Gras)

Daily . . . . 9 am - 5 pm

Cost

Adults $7
Students 13 - 18 . . . . $4
Children 6 - 12 . . . . $4

Directions

From New Orleans, take I-10 west to exit #194 (Gramercy) and go left on Highway 641 (south). Highway 641 will become Highway 3213. Continue on and cross over the Veteran's Memorial Bridge. Go left onto Highway 18. Continue 3½ miles to the plantation.

OAK ALLEY PLANTATION

3645 LA Highway 18 • Vacherie, Louisiana 70090
800-442-5539 or 225-265-2151

Picturesque, magnificent old oak trees

You're already familiar with this plantation. You've seen it numerous times in movies, documentaries, and photographs. Oak Alley's famous for its canopy of old live oak trees—14 on each side—leading to the elegant Greek Revival mansion. The trees, believed to be over 300 years old, were planted by a French settler in the early 1700's.

The plantation offers tours of the mansion daily, every 30 minutes. Tours last 40 minutes. Docents dress in antebellum attire. Visitors are welcome to walk the grounds any time. Be sure to browse through the nifty gift shop. The Oak Alley Restaurant serves tasty Creole and Cajun breakfasts and lunches. A great place to eat. You'll find the five comfy Creole bed and breakfast cottages at the plantation a delightful place to stay.

Hours

(Closed Thanksgiving and Christmas)
November - February (Last tour at 5 pm)
Daily . . . . 9 am - 5 pm
March - October (Last tour at 5:30 pm)
Daily . . . . 9 am - 5:30 pm

Cost

Adults $8
Children . . . . 6-12 yrs . . $3; 13-18 yrs . .$5

Directions

From New Orleans, take I-10 west to exit #194 (Gramercy) and go left on Hwy 641 (south). Hwy 641 will become Hwy 3213. Cross over the Veteran's Memorial Bridge. Go left onto Hwy 18. Continue 7 ½ miles.

TEZCUCO PLANTATION

3138 Highway 44 River Road
Darrow, Louisiana 70725 • 225-562-3929

Old plantation home and museum with unique artifacts

The highpoint of your visit to the Tezcuco plantation will be the River Road African/American Museum and Gallery. Unique in what it has to offer, the museum's artifacts include tools used by workers on the plantation, old photographs of slaves, Confederate soldiers, jazz musicians, old African musical instruments and documents for purchasing and emancipating slaves. The museum is open Wednesday - Saturday 10 am - 5 pm, Sunday 1 pm - 5 pm. Admission is free. 225-644-7955

A tour of the house will give you a look into the height of the antebellum period just before the Civil War. Built in 1855, the house is furnished with one of the finest collection of furnishings from that period. The house is listed on the National Register of Historic Places. Guides take you through the house dressed in antebellum attire.

Hours
(Closed Thanksgiving, Christmas, and New Year's Eve)
Daily . . . . 9 am - 5 pm

Cost
Adults $7
Children (13-18) $6
Children (4-12) $3.25
Seniors $6

Directions
Located 1 hour from New Orleans. Take I-10 west and exit 179 onto LA 44 going south. Go 5½ miles to Burnside. Will be 1 mile north of the Sunshine Bridge on LA 44.

HOUMAS HOUSE PLANTATION AND GARDENS

40136 Highway 942
Darrow, Louisiana 70725
225-473-7841 or 888-323-8314

Once the state's largest sugar cane plantation

Two early settlers, Maurice Conway and Alexandre Latil, bought this tract of land from the Houmas Indians in the early 1700's to raise sugar cane. Much later, in 1840, owner John Smith Preston built the plantation's Greek Revival mansion. Fortunately, the mansion survived the Civil War. The owner then, John Burnside, was a native of Ireland who declared immunity as a British subject. After the war, under the ownership of Colonel Williams, the plantation thrived as the largest producer of sugar in the state. He produced over 20 million pounds a year.

The mansion is completely restored and furnished with period antiques. Take the guided tour with tour guides dressed in antebellum attire. Surrounding the mansion are lovely gardens. The mansion was the setting for the movie *Hush, Hush, Sweet Charlotte*.

Hours

Daily (Feb.- Oct.) . . . . 10 am - 5 pm
Daily (Nov.-Jan.) . . . . 10 am - 4 pm

Cost

Adults $8
Children (13-17) $6
Children (6-12) $3

Directions

Take I-10 west to exit 179 and continue on Hwy 44 south to Burnside. Turn right on LA 942 and go ½ mile to the plantation.

MADEWOOD PLANTATION HOUSE

4250 Highway 308
Napoleonville, Louisiana 70390
225-369-7151 or 800-375-7151

Candlelight dinner with overnight stays

Experience a thrilling overnight stay in one of Madewood's eight bedrooms with canopied beds and antebellum furnishings. Eat dinner by candlelight around the huge oak table in the dining room. The food's delicious—gumbo, shrimp pie, pumpkin Lafourche and cornbread.

Built in 1846, Madewood is one of the largest plantation homes in Louisiana. The owner constructed the mansion from trees on the property, hence the name Madewood. The house is listed on the National Registry of Historic Places. Take the tour of the mansion.

Hours

Daily .... 10 am - 4:30 pm

Cost

Adults $6
Students/Children (8-18) $4
Seniors $5
One night's stay $225

Directions

Located 2 miles south of Napoleonville on Highway 308.

NOTTOWAY PLANTATION

30970 Highway 405
White Castle, Louisiana 70788
225-545-2730

The largest plantation home in the South

Although Emily Randolph was home alone with her children and a couple of slaves, she kept the Union soldiers out of her home. Surrounding plantation homes had been looted and burned. Determined that this wouldn't happen to hers, she succeeded in fighting them off. Her story of courage inspired the novel *Gone with the Wind*.

Nottoway Plantation is definitely worth a visit. Built in 1859, it was innovative for its day, with indoor plumbing and (hot and cold) running water.

Take a tour of the house. A highlight of Nottoway is the experience of staying overnight in one of the elegant bedrooms.

Hours

(Closed Christmas Day)

Daily . . . . 9 am - 5 pm

Cost

Adults $10
Children 6 - 12 . . . . $4
Children under 5 . . . . Free
One night's stay . . . . $125-$250

Directions

Located one hour from New Orleans. Take I-10 west and exit LA 22. Go left on LA 70 across the Sunshine Bridge and continue 14 miles north through Donaldsonville on Highway 1. Watch for signs.

Bayou Country - Baton Rouge
LOUISIANA STATE UNIVERSITY RURAL LIFE MUSEUM AND WINDRUSH GARDENS

4650 Essen Lane
Baton Rouge, Louisiana 70809
225-765-2437

Pre-industrial Southern Louisiana

As a tribute to the common folks of southern Louisiana, the Rural Life Museum demonstrates the lifestyle of the laboring class during the plantation era. Watch the 5-minute video before exploring the museum and grounds. The complex has three sections: the barn, the working plantation, and the folk architecture. It takes 2 to 3 hours to see it all. Guided tours are available. Interesting. Very educational. A must-do. After that, wander through the lovely semi-formal gardens with winding paths and lakes adjacent to the museum complex. Mr. Steele Burden, the late former owner whose family donated the property to the museum, was a landscape architect.

Hours

Daily . . . . 8:30 am - 5 pm

Cost

Adults $5
Children 5 - 11 . . . . $3
Children under 5 . . . . Free
Seniors $4

Directions

Located at I-10 and Essen Street.

Bayou Country - Breaux Bridge
MULATE'S CAJUN RESTAURANT

325 Mills Street
Breaux Bridge, LA 70517
337-332-4648 or 800-422-2586

Cajun eatery and dance hall

Real Cajun stuff: red and white checked plastic table cloths, alligator hides tacked on the wall, an old cypress dance floor, and live Cajun music. Their specialties are fried seafood—alligator, catfish, frog legs—and crawfish mania. In fact, the town of Breaux Bridge calls itself the "Crawfish Capital of the World."

An age-old institution for families, Mulate's dance floor of cypress wood dates back 5 generations. Cajun bands play nightly and during lunch on weekends. Come dressed casually and *laissez les bon temps rouler*.

Hours

Winter hours vary; call ahead

Mon. - Thurs.	11 am - 10 pm
Fri. and Sat.	11 am - 10:30 pm

Cost

Average for entrees $14.95

Directions

From I-10 take exit 109 and go south on Hwy 328 to Breaux Bridge. Turn right on Hwy 94. Mulate's will be on your left.

Cajun Country - Sunset
CHRETIAN POINT PLANTATION

665 Chretian Point Road
Sunset, Louisiana 70584
800-880-7050 or 337-662-5876

Spend the night in an elegant plantation home

It's the fabulous staircase in the rear hallway that makes Chretian Point plantation an important stop. Filmmakers copied the staircase for Tara in the movie *Gone with the Wind*. Built in 1831, the elegant old mansion fell into disrepair after the Civil War. It now is completely restored and full of marvelous antiques from its heyday. Note the lunettes over the doorway and windows; they're patterned after those in the Palace of Versailles in France. Once part of a 10,000-acre cotton plantation, the house now serves as a bed and breakfast, with 4 bedrooms and a master bedroom suite. Prices for overnight stays range from $95-225 and include a plantation breakfast. This elegant old plantation home is now listed on the National Register of Historic Places.

Hours for tour
(Closed most holidays)

Daily . . . . 10 am - 5 pm

Cost

Adults $6.50
Children under 12 . . . . $3

Directions

From I-10 take exit #97 and go north through Ossun, Vatican, and Cankton (approx. 8 miles). 2.2 miles north of Cankton, turn left on Parish Road 356 toward Bristol. Go one block, turn right on Chretian Point Road. Go one mile. Will be on the left.

Cajun Country - Lafayette
ACADIAN CULTURAL CENTER, JEAN LAFITTE NATIONAL PARK

501 Fisher Road
Lafayette, Louisiana 70508
337-232-0789

Learn about the Acadian history and culture

Make this a stop on your way through Lafayette. The Acadian Cultural Center focuses on the people who settled southern Louisiana in the late 1700's. Having lived in Nova Scotia for over a hundred years, the Acadians were driven out by the British. The center tells their story in a 45-minute video—a must see. Well done.

The center features a collection of artifacts and explores the different aspects of their culture: their cuisine, clothing, home furnishings, farming, music, language, architecture, and religion. The center also sells a variety of books and music CDs.

Hours
Closed Christmas Day
Daily .... 8 am - 5 pm
Video starts on the hour .... 9 am - 4 pm

Cost
Free

Directions

From I-10 take exit 103-A and go south on Evangeline Thruway. Turn left on Surrey St. The Lafayette Regional Airport will be on your right and immediately past the airport on the left will be Fisher Road. Turn left and it will be on the right.

Cajun Country - Lafayette
ACADIAN VILLAGE

200 Greenleaf Road
Lafayette, Louisiana 70506
337-981-2364 or 800-962-9133

Life as it was in the late 1800's in southern Louisiana

Visit a re-created Acadian village. See what it was like to live in southern Louisiana in the 19th century. Located on 10 lush acres of trees and gardens, the village consists of 11 original settlers' homes, a museum, and the Rodrique Gallery. The Rodrique paintings depict incidents of Acadian history—their expulsion from Nova Scotia, the journey to Louisiana, and more. The artist Rodrique, a native of the area, is famous for his Blue Dog paintings.

Visitors guide themselves through the village after a brief docent introduction.

Hours

Closed New Year's Day, Mardi Gras, Easter Sunday, and Thanksgiving
Daily . . . . 10 am - 5 pm

Cost

Adults $6
Children 6 - 14 . . . . $2.50
Seniors $5

Directions

From I-10, take exit 100 and go south on Ambassador Caffery Road. Turn right on Ridge Road, the left on W. Broussard. Will be on the left.

Cajun Country - Lafayette
PREJEAN'S RESTAURANT

3480 I-49 North
Lafayette, Louisiana 70507
337-896-3247

Cajun food at its finest

Their award-winning chef grew up in Montana, but he knows how Cajun food's cooked. Food here is to die for and the menus 7 pages long. If you're indecisive, try one of their seafood platter entrees. House favorites like the Pan Sautéed Red Snapper loaded with crawfish, crab, and artichoke cream sauce or the Pepper Jack Shrimp stuffed with Jack cheese and taco, wrapped with applewood smoked bacon and topped with crawfish cardinale will simply have to wait your return. And then there's the dessert tray.

Listen to live Cajun music while you dine. The dress is dressy casual.

Hours

Sun. - Thurs. . . . . II am - I0 pm
Fri. and Sat. . . . . II am - II pm

Cost

Entrees $14.95-24.95

Directions

From I-10 take exit 103-B to I-49 North. Prejean's is on the right two miles north of I-10 on I-49.

Cajun Country - Lafayette
VERMILIONVILLE

1600 Surrey St.
Lafayette, Louisiana 70508
337-233-4077 or 800-99 BAYOU
www.vermilionville.org

A recreated Acadian village on Bayou Vermilion

Driven from their homes in Nova Scotia in 1755 for refusing to swear allegiance to the British, the Acadians finally settled in southern Louisiana. These immigrants settled along Bayous and the prairie lands. One of those settlements was called Vermilionville, located on Bayou Vermilion. Today, the site of that small town is a living museum dedicated to preserving the early Acadians' culture.

Have a true experience in Acadian folklore. Wander through Vermilionville, a re-created Acadian village, demonstrating cooking, blacksmithing, doll-making, weaving, spinning, boat building, and more. Live music everyday. Authenticity's the word. Guided tours available. Plan to spend 1 1/2 to 2 hours. Live Cajun music, restaurant, and art gallery.

Hours

Closed Christmas and New Year's Day

Daily . . . . 10 am - 5 pm

Cost

Adults $8
Seniors $6.50
Children 6 - 12 . . . . $5
Children under 6 . . . . Free

Directions

Located next to the Acadian Cultural Center-Jean Lafitte National Park.

Bayou Country - New Iberia
RIP VAN WINKLE GARDENS ON JEFFERSON ISLAND

5505 Rip Van Winkle Road
New Iberville, Louisiana 70560
337-365-3332 or 800-375-3332

Enjoy beauty and serenity

Joseph Jefferson, who's famed for portraying Rip Van Winkle, bought Jefferson Island in 1865 as a winter retreat. Surrounded by marshland and Lake Peigneur, Jefferson Island—not really an island but a salt dome—creates the perfect serene oasis. Here he built his magnificent Georgian estate with 20 acres of landscaped gardens.

Although the gardens bloom year round, springtime is the best. Over 50,000 tulips, hyacinths, daffodils, and azaleas explode with color. Take a guided tour of the home, stroll through the gardens, and take a boat excursion on Lake Peigneur. The gardens include a restaurant, gift shop, convention center, theater, and a bed and breakfast cottage.

Hours

Daily . . . . 9 am - 5 pm

Cost (including tour of house)

Adults $9
Student $7
Children under 12 . . . . $5
Seniors $8.50

Directions

From I-10 take exit 103-A through Lafayette on US Hwy 90 towards New Iberia. Turn right on Hwy 14. Turn right on Rip Van Winkle Road to Jefferson Island.

Bayou Country - New Iberia
CONRAD RICE MILLS/ KONDRIKO COMPANY STORE

307 Ann St.
New Iberville, Louisiana 70560
337-367-6163 or 800-551-3245

Visit the oldest rice mill in America

Take a tour through the old rice mill located in the heart of Cajun country. Not only will you tour the oldest rice mill in the country, you'll have a Cajun experience. The tour begins with a 20-minute slide show in the Kondriko Company Store. The show tells you about the Cajun culture and the surrounding area. Learn about the planting, the harvesting, and the different varieties of rice available. Then walk through the old rice mill and watch them packaging the rice. They'll explain how they season the different rice packages and give details about some of their products. The tour lasts 40 minutes. Very informative. After the tour, browse through the store's selection of regional food products and souvenirs for the trip back home.

Hours
Mon. - Sat.	9 am - 5 pm
Tours	10 & 11am, 1, 2, & 3pm

Cost
Adults	$2.75
Children under 12	$1.25
Seniors	$2.25

Directions
From I-10 take exit 103-A through Lafayette on US Hwy 90 to New Iberia. Turn left on Hwy 14 toward New Iberia (Center St.). Continue 3 miles to St. Peter St. Turn right and go 3 blocks. Turn right on Ann St. Will be on the left.

Coastal Country - Avery Island
JUNGLE GARDENS AND BIRD CITY

Highway 329
Avery Island, Louisiana 70513
337-369-6243

Beautiful tropical plants and birds on Avery Island

The Tabasco Sauce founder's son, E. A. McIlhenny, built a 200-acre sanctuary for birds on Avery Island. As a naturalist, he took interest in saving the snowy egret from extinction in the late 19th century. He searched for enough birds to finally make a colony. Nowadays over 20,000 snowy egrets and other birds nest each year on a special platform built for them and known as Bird City.

Enjoy the serenity of the gardens. See an abundance of wildlife: deer, black bears, nutrias, raccoons, and alligators.

Hours
Daily .... 8 am - 5 pm

Cost
Adults $5.75
Children (6-12) $4

Directions

From I-10 going west, exit the Lafayette/U.S. Highway 90 and go south through Lafayette and New Iberia. Exit LA 14 and go left. At the LA 329 junction, turn right. Continue on LA 329 to Avery Island.

Coastal Country - Avery Island
TABASCO PEPPER SAUCE FACTORY

Avery Island, Louisiana 70513
337-373-6120

Famous sauce-making factory near New Iberia

Tabasco Sauce: you've used it to spice-up all sorts of foods. Now visit the plant that makes it. Edmund McIlhenny, during the post-Civil War era, created the product. Made from the Capsicum pepper, the recipe is patented. Today, the peppers not only grow on Avery Island—a huge salt dome surrounded with water and marshland—but in several South American countries too. Tour the factory and see how the peppers are processed into Tabasco Sauce. Free recipes and samples.

Hours

(Closed Sundays, holidays and some three-day weekends)

Mon. - Fri . . . . 9 am - 4 pm
Saturday . . . . 9 am - Noon

Cost
Free

Directions

From I-10 going west, exit the Lafayette/U.S. Highway 90 and go south through Lafayette and New Iberia. Exit LA 14 and go left. At the LA 329 junction, turn right. Continue on LA 329 to Avery Island.

Symbols

A

B

Index

TOPP KNOTCH
P E R S O N N E L   I N C

"Your Global Staffing Resource"

 # 2 Canal Street * Suite 2610 * New Orleans, La 70130
Phone (504) 524-8574 * Fax (504) 524-6876
Toll Free 1-866-744-8677

Hi Yvonne!

We're looking forward to seeing you. Hope this Book helps.

See you Soon!

Love
Dana

Copy and mail this form with your check to:

Into Fun, Company Publications
Order Form

P.O. Box 2494, Sugar Land, Texas 77487-2494
281-980-9745 • Fax: 281-494-9745
www.intofun.com

**Cost per
T-shirt:
$12.95**

Call for information
on purchasing INTO
FUN T-shirts.

Please send me
142 Fun Things To Do In New Orleans:

Total # Books_____ @$12.95 each = $_____

Shipping, Handling: $4.25 + 8.25% sales tax = $_____

Total included $_____

Send to:

Name _____

Company Name _____

Mailing address _____

_____

City/ State/ Zip _____

_____

Phone _____